FOOTBALL
NOW!

FOOTBALL NOW!

THIRD EDITION

MIKE RYAN

Firefly Books

A FIREFLY BOOK

Published by Firefly Books Ltd. 2012

Copyright © 2012 Firefly Books Ltd.

Text copyright © 2012 Mike Ryan
Images copyright as listed on this page

First printing

Publisher Cataloging-in-Publication Data (U.S.)
Ryan, Mike.
    Football now! / Ryan, Mike.
3rd ed.
[176] p. : col. ill. ; cm.
Includes index.
ISBN-13: 978-1-55407-884-4 (pbk.)
1. National Football League -- Biography.
2. Football players -- Biography.
I. Title.
796.332/092 B dc23   GV939.5.A1R936   2012

Library and Archives Canada Cataloguing in Publication Ryan, Mike, 1974- Football now! / Mike Ryan. -- 3rd ed. Includes index. Previous eds. by Mike Leonetti and John Iaboni. ISBN 978-1-55407-884-4
1. Football players--United States--Biography. 2. National Football League--Biography. 3. Football players--United States-- Pictorial works. 4. National Football League--Pictorial works. I. Title.
GV939.A1R93 2012   796.332092'2   C2012-902186-5

Published in the United States by
Firefly Books (U.S.) Inc.
P.O. Box 1338, Ellicott Station
Buffalo, New York 14205

Published in Canada by
Firefly Books Ltd.
66 Leek Crescent
Richmond Hill, Ontario L4B 1H1

Cover and interior design: Luna Design

Printed in Canada

The publisher gratefully acknowledges the financial support for our publishing program by the Government of Canada through the Canada Book Fund as administered by the Department of Canadian Heritage.

For little Charlie — future Iowa Hawkeye and Chicago Bear — and Cheryl and big Charlie, who showed me that real heroes are sometimes closer than you think.

Contents

Introduction

The summer before the 2011 NFL season was a dark one for football fans. The owners had locked out the players, who in turn sued the owners. At a time when the American economy was receding and unemployment and home foreclosures were climbing, a battle between millionaires and billionaires acting in their own self-interest seemed thoughtless and out of touch with reality.

With the season in jeopardy, it looked as though it would be the fans who would be the ultimate loser in the fight. But, at the 11th hour the players and the owners came to an agreement, and after an abbreviated training camp there was a full season of football. But how would the fans react? And with such little preparation time, what would the quality of football be like?

Turns out the fans returned in droves and were treated to one of the most exciting football seasons in history.

The 2011 season became known as the Year of the Quarterback. In the history of the NFL only five men have thrown for over 5,000 yards in a season, and three of them did it in 2011. Drew Brees ultimately topped Tom Brady after both broke Dan Marino's 27-year-old single-season record of 5,084 passing yards, while Matthew Stafford came just shy of the Marino mark. Aaron Rodgers may not have thrown for 5,000-plus yards, but he was named the NFL's MVP after a near perfect season. Second-year quarterback Tim Tebow became one of the most famous men in America as "Tebowmania" and "Tebowing" entered the pop culture vernacular and his stirring fourth-quarter comebacks became the stuff of legend (despite stats that only a mother could love). Cam Newton put together the best rookie season a quarterback has ever had, while veteran Peyton Manning managed to dominate headlines even though he sat out the entire season recovering from neck surgery. In the end it was Peyton's younger brother, Eli, who performed the best when it mattered most, winning his second Lombardi Trophy and Super Bowl MVP award after upsetting Brady and the New England Patriots for the second time in four years.

However, it wasn't all about the quarterbacks in 2011. In fact, their favorite targets — the freakishly athletic and increasingly important tight ends — had a banner year too.

In New Orleans, rookie Jimmy Graham had one of the most impressive seasons ever played at the position, but his sophomore counterpart in New England, Rob Gronkowski, upstaged him as he shattered the tight end touchdown record.

On the defensive side of the ball, Jared Allen came within half a sack of tying the single-season record. Graybeards Charles Woodson and Ray Lewis continued to lead their teams on the field and in the dressing room, while young defensive stars like Von Miller and Jason Pierre-Paul emerged.

The storylines didn't dry up in the offseason, either. The Indianapolis Colts cut ties with Peyton Manning after 13 consecutive years of stellar football; the Colts then drafted quarterback Andrew Luck first overall to replace him. Manning, being courted by most of the league, chose to go to the Denver Broncos, leading the Broncos to trade Tebow to the New York Jets and igniting an instant quarterback controversy in America's media center.

And swirling beneath all of it was the bounty scandal of the New Orleans Saints. With the city preparing to host Super Bowl XLVII at the end of the 2012 season, several of the club's coaches and players, as well as the general manager, received supplementary discipline for a bounty program in which players were rewarded for injuring opponents.

These narratives and superstars make football the most popular, influential, controversial and highest grossing sport in America. The 77 players presented in *Football Now!* are the best in the league, and they represent every part of the country: rundown Rust Belt towns, inner cities, affluent suburbs and dusty rural outposts. They come from football royalty, major colleges, tiny community schools and broken homes. There are undersized overachievers and those with superhuman size and athleticism; grizzled veterans, young hotshots, medical miracles and emotional leaders.

What they all have in common is that they give fans and communities something to rally around. From September to February fans show up, tune in and log on to see their favorite team wage battle in the NFL's drama of brutality, frailty, loss and triumph. Football is a violent game, but at its highest level it's a thing of beauty, played by some of the most highly-skilled and talented athletes in the world.

These are the players, and here are their stories.

SAM BRADFORD — St. Louis Rams

TOM BRADY — New England Patriots

DREW BREES — New Orleans Saints

JAY CUTLER — Chicago Bears

ANDY DALTON — Cincinnati Bengals

ELI MANNING — New York Giants

PEYTON MANNING — Denver Broncos

CAM NEWTON — Carolina Panthers

PHILIP RIVERS — San Diego Chargers

BEN ROETHLISBERGER — Pittsburgh Steelers

AARON RODGERS — Green Bay Packers

TONY ROMO — Dallas Cowboys

MATT RYAN — Atlanta Falcons

MARK SANCHEZ — New York Jets

MATT STAFFORD — Detroit Lions

TIM TEBOW — New York Jets

MICHAEL VICK — Philadelphia Eagles

QUARTERBACKS

ST. LOUIS RAMS

★ ★ ★

QUARTERBACK

8

SAM BRADFORD

Growing up in Oklahoma City, Oklahoma, Sam Bradford seemed destined for greatness. Bradford was the son of an offensive lineman who played for Barry Switzer at the University of Oklahoma in the 1970s, so there was little doubt that Sam would follow his father Kent's footsteps to Norman. The question was which sport would he choose?

In high school, Bradford was a quarterback and a scratch golfer, and he averaged a double-double with his basketball team. According to teammate and NBA Rookie of the Year Blake Griffin, "He was good — really good,

actually. He could shoot, he could pass, he could do it all."

Despite his athletic prowess and success as a high school quarterback, Bradford wasn't a highly recruited prospect, and he arrived in Oklahoma in 2006 low on the QB depth chart. Senior Paul Thompson led the team that season, but his graduation left a void, and while six players tried out for his position, Bradford was the one who won the job.

It didn't take him long to prove he belonged. In his first game he set the school record for passing in a half with 363

yards, and in his second game Bradford broke Heisman Trophy–winner Jason White's school record for most consecutive pass completions with 22.

IN THE HUDDLE
Bradford is 1/16 Cherokee, and was the first Heisman Trophy winner of Native American heritage.

In Bradford's sophomore season he set the school record for passing yards in a game (468), helped the Sooners break the University of Hawaii's record for points in a single season (702) and led the way for the Sooners to become the first team in NCAA history to score 60 or more points in five consecutive games.

These accomplishments did not go unnoticed by Heisman voters, and Bradford was only the second sophomore to win the trophy. He narrowly beat out Tim Tebow, who was the first sophomore winner the year prior.

With little left to accomplish in college football, many expected Bradford to declare for the draft. For Bradford, however, one major accomplishment was missing — a national championship — and he was determined to win it.

Life has a funny way of

CAREER HIGHLIGHTS

- First overall pick in the 2010 draft
- Signed the largest rookie contract in NFL history
- Broke Peyton Manning's record for most completed passes by an NFL rookie quarterback (326)
- While at Oklahoma became the second sophomore in history to win the Heisman Trophy (after Tim Tebow)
- Holds the NCAA record for most touchdown passes (36) by a freshman quarterback

messing with best-laid plans, though, and in the first game of Bradford's junior year, one play after becoming the Sooners' all-time passing leader, he sustained a third-degree sprain of the AC joint in his throwing shoulder. Deciding to take the rehab route instead of surgery, Bradford was back at the helm three weeks later, throwing for 389 yards in a blowout win over Baylor University. One week after that, in a game against the University of Texas, Bradford was driven to the ground in the first quarter, suffering a third-degree shoulder separation, which put an end to his college career and possibly to his dream of becoming an NFL quarterback.

Bradford underwent surgery and began a grueling nine-week rehab assignment. When it was time to throw again, his first attempt traveled all of 10 yards. Bradford persevered and he gradually gained strength and distance. His first real test was Pro Day, with scouts from 21 teams there to watch a private workout. Bradford passed with flying colors, completing 63 of

64 passes and vaulting to the top of the draft class.

It's one thing, however, to excel in the controlled environment of Pro Day versus an actual NFL game that's spent facing down 300-pound men who are bent on slamming their opponents into the turf. At 6-foot-4 and 228 pounds, Bradford and his surgically repaired shoulder held up to the rigors of his rookie season with the St. Louis Rams, who took him first overall in the 2010 draft.

In his first eight games, Bradford had 11 TDs, which tied an NFL record held by Dan Marino (1983), Peyton Manning (1998) and Ben Roethlisberger (2004). During October and November, he also set a record for most consecutive passes

without an interception for a rookie (169), and on December 26, he topped Manning for most passes completed by a rookie (326).

Bradford finished the season with 354 completions on 590 throws, surpassing Manning's record of 575 for most attempts by a rookie quarterback. He also became just the third rookie to start all 16 regular-season games and pass for over 3,000 yards. Bradford topped it all off with the Offensive Rookie of the Year Award.

An ankle injury limited Bradford's effectiveness and playing time in 2011, but in 2012, fantasy football players will be wise to invest in him while Rams fans remain confident they have a bull going forward.

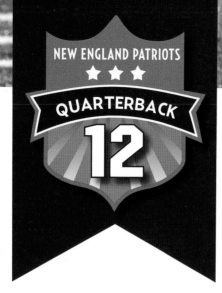

TOM BRADY

Tom Brady has officially crossed over into the mainstream — people who don't know a touchdown from a touch screen now recognize him for his matinee-idol looks, his endorsements, his relationships and his regular appearance on the covers of magazines at the grocery checkout.

The tabloids didn't appear to be in Brady's future when he was growing up in San Mateo, California, but it's possible that his path to football stardom began as early as four years old, which was when he sat in the stands and watched one of the most famous touchdowns in NFL history — Joe Montana's pass to Dwight Clark for "The Catch" that sent the 49ers to the Super Bowl in 1982.

Montana is the quarterback Brady is most often compared to, and, says Brett Favre, "The way he plays, mechanically speaking, and how sound he is in his decision-making, it seems like he never puts himself or his team in a bad position … he reminds me a lot of Joe Montana."

Soft-spoken, just as Montana was, Brady has an inner fire that has fueled his success, and it is one that was stoked while he played at the University of Michigan. Considered skinny and slow, he was hardly the toast of Ann Arbor. Brady, however, developed faith in his ability, as well as a capacity

CAREER HIGHLIGHTS

- Two-time NFL MVP (2007, 2010) and the first unanimous MVP selection in NFL history (2010)
- Three-time Super Bowl champion (XXXVII, XXXVIII, XXXIX)
- Two-time Super Bowl MVP (XXXVII, XXXVIII)
- Three-time All-Pro (2005, 2007, 2010)
- Seven-time Pro Bowl selection (2001, 2004, 2005, 2007, 2009–2011)
- NFL All-Decade Team for the 2000s
- Comeback Player of the Year (2009)
- *Sports Illustrated* Sportsman of the Year (2005)
- Holds the single-season record for most touchdowns in a season (50) and the longest streak without an interception (335 attempts)

to ignore detractors. He focused on winning over his teammates instead of fans and he learned to use slights as motivation. His penchant for patience paid off after he waited until the sixth round to be drafted by the New England Patriots, 199th overall, in 2000.

Brady took the league by storm and by the end of the 2001–2002 season was New England's starting quarterback, Super Bowl champion and Super Bowl MVP.

Following the 2003 and 2004 seasons, the Patriots won the Super Bowl again, with Brady picking up the game's MVP award in the 2003 championship.

In 2007, it looked as if the Patriots were on their way to their fourth Super Bowl of the decade after Brady set an NFL single-season record with 50 touchdowns, won his first MVP award and led the team to a perfect 16–0 record in the regular season … but a funny thing happened on the way to immortality. Behind Eli Manning and one of the most unlikely and amazing catches in NFL history, the New York Giants upset the Patriots to win Super Bowl XLII 17–14.

Following this loss, in the first game of the 2008 season, Brady suffered a devastating knee injury that cost him a year of football, but he came back strong in 2009, and in 2010, he became the first player in NFL history to be unanimously selected as league MVP.

In 2011, Brady somehow achieved yet another level of success, throwing for 5,235 yards to break Dan Marino's 1984 single-season yardage record. It was the year of the quarterback, however, and he finished behind Drew Brees of the New Orleans Saints, who had 5,476 yards.

IN THE HUDDLE

Brady's overall record in the regular season and playoffs is 138–40 for a .775 winning percentage, which is the best of any quarterback in the Super Bowl era (the years including and following 1966).

Brady, however, was better when it counted, and the Patriots made it to the Super Bowl in a highly anticipated rematch with the Giants; it was Brady's chance for revenge and a 17th postseason win that would break his tie with Montana.

Super Bowl XLVI was a seesaw affair that went down to the last play, and in the end, the conclusion was a bitter pill for Brady to swallow — he had the ball in his hand and a chance to win with just under a minute left, but his Hail Mary pass on the final play was batted down and the game was over.

For the second time in four years, Manning and the Giants had narrowly beat Brady's Patriots, keeping him — yet again — from fully solidifying his NFL legacy. Additionally, the headlines were less than kind after Brady's supermodel wife Gisele Bündchen publicly defended him and deflected blame immediately after the game.

Much of the venom was surely based on jealousy of the pair's charmed life together, but Brady, true to form, wouldn't bite, which means he will just file everything away for positive motivation in the coming season — funny how that works.

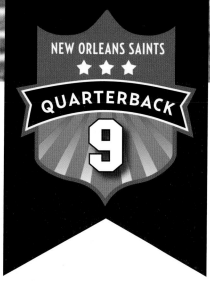

NEW ORLEANS SAINTS
QUARTERBACK
9

DREW BREES

The man and the city needed each other; both were battered and bruised with a future that looked bleak, but America, built on tales of redemption, loves a second act.

On the final day of 2005, Drew Brees, quarterback for the San Diego Chargers, suffered a torn labrum and rotator cuff in his throwing shoulder. He underwent a successful surgery but his football future was in jeopardy, especially considering the fact that the Chargers already had their quarterback of the future, Philip Rivers, waiting in the wings. Indeed, Brees' fate was sealed and he was released from the team.

Earlier that year, in August, the city of New Orleans had been torn apart by Hurricane Katrina. The city was in shambles, the confirmed death toll was close to 2,000 and the Superdome, home of the Saints, became a symbol of the city's darkest hour when people huddled there throughout the storm.

In the aftermath, the Saints played the majority of their home games at Louisiana State University in Baton Rouge and at the Alamodome in San Antonio, Texas. The sense of displacement showed — the club struggled to a 3–13 record in 2005. The off-season, however, provided the Saints with a chance to redeem a down-and-out quarterback in need of a team to believe in him. "It was a calling," according to Brees. "[My wife and I] were brought here for a reason."

At a time when New Orleans felt abandoned by the country, Brees and his wife Brittany embraced the city, rebuilding an old home in the north end and becoming visibly active in the community. After arriving, they set up The Brees Dream Foundation to help fight cancer and provide "care, education and opportunities for children in need," which includes building playgrounds and repairing football fields in the downtown area.

IN THE HUDDLE

In 2011, Brees set the record for single-season passing yards (5,476), most completions in a season (468), most consecutive 300-plus yard passing games (7), most consecutive games with 350-plus yards passing (4) and highest completion percentage for a season (71.2 percent).

"He symbolizes the people of New Orleans in many, many ways," says NFL commissioner Roger Goodell. "Drew believes in that community. He believes in doing what's right. He's one of the most genuine people I've ever met."

Brees is also a leader on the field, and after joining a team that had been mired in mediocrity for many years (they were often

CAREER HIGHLIGHTS

- Six-time Pro Bowl selection (2004, 2006, 2008, 2009, 2010, 2011)
- Four-time All-Pro (2006, 2008, 2009, 2011)
- Two-time Offensive Player of the Year (2008, 2011)
- Super Bowl XLIV MVP (2010)
- *Sports Illustrated* Sportsman of the Year (2010)
- NFL Comeback Player of the Year (2004)
- The only player in NFL history with two seasons of 5,000+ yards passing (2008, 2011)
- Currently second all-time with an active streak of 43 games with at least one touchdown pass (Brees needs five more to break Johnny Unitas' record)
- First recipient of the Socrates Award, which recognizes the NCAA's best athlete in terms of academics, athletics and community service

referred to as the "'Aints"), he came in and led the team to a 10–6 record in his first season, marching them all the way to the NFC Championship, which they lost to the Chicago Bears.

The city suddenly had something to rally around, and the culmination of all that civic pride came on February 7, 2010, when Brees tied a Super Bowl record with 32 completions and took home the MVP award as the Saints beat the Indianapolis Colts 31–17 in Super Bowl XLIV to win the franchise's first championship, setting off one of the biggest parties in the history of a town known for its revelry.

In 2011, Brees had one of the most prolific seasons in NFL history. He won the Offensive Player of the Year Award after breaking one of the most iconic

records in the game (Dan Marino's 27-year-old single-season record for passing yards), which he did with a game to spare, finishing the season with 5,476 yards, 241 yards more than Tom Brady, who also broke Marino's record. Brees also set records for completions in a season (468) and completion percentage (71.2 percent) while throwing 46 touchdowns.

Brees' aerial assault in 2011 led to his ownership of just about every record in the Saints' book, as well as several NFL single-season records. He also achieved a division title with a 13–3 record, and in the playoffs threw for over 460 yards in each game the Saints played, racking up a total of 7 touchdowns and a quarterback rating of 110.1. After beating the Detroit Lions

45–28 in the wildcard game and looking unstoppable on offense, the Saints ran into one of the league's best defenses in the San Francisco 49ers. Brees had 40 completions and 4 touchdowns against the 49ers in the NFC divisional playoff, but he was sacked three times and intercepted twice as the Saints lost 36–32.

The people of New Orleans, however, will be ready to put on a show when Super Bowl XLVII comes to town following the 2012 season. The newly named Mercedes-Benz Superdome will be the biggest, glitziest stage in the country, and if Brees can lead the Saints to victory in a city that had been written off — and in the stadium that once housed its misery — it will be the ultimate American comeback story.

CHICAGO BEARS
★ ★ ★

QUARTERBACK

6

JAY CUTLER

In 2011 *Sports Illustrated* published an article entitled "You're Wrong About Jay Cutler," and it summed up the life and times of the Chicago Bears quarterback, who carries himself with an aloof demeanor, keeping a distance from the fans who want to know their heroes intimately.

"He just really doesn't care what other people think," explains Cutler's Heritage Hills High School coach, Bob Clayton. "That pisses people off."

Clayton tried to get the kid from Santa Claus, Indiana, to be a more demonstrative leader, but, as the numbers show, he didn't have to do much to make Cutler an effective quarterback — the team went 15–0 in his senior year, outscoring opponents 746–85 before winning the state championship.

Cutler went on to Vanderbilt University, where he set 22 school records, including total offense (9,953 yards), passing yards (8,697), touchdowns (59), completions (710), combined touchdowns (76) and completions without an interception (167).

Drafted 11th overall in the 2006 draft by the Denver Broncos, Cutler was the heir apparent to Hall of

CAREER HIGHLIGHTS

- Holds the Denver Broncos' franchise records for single-season passing yards (4,526), completions (384) and 300+ yard passing games (8)
- 2008 Pro Bowl selection
- First-team All-SEC (2005)
- SEC Offensive Player of the Year (2005)

Famer John Elway, and he lived up to the hype immediately, throwing 50 touchdowns in only 33 games (quicker than any other Bronco) and becoming the first quarterback in NFL history with multiple touchdown throws in his first four games.

In 2008, Cutler became the third quarterback in NFL history with a 4,500-yard passing season in his first three years in the league, and at that point was also already second in Broncos history in completions and fifth in passing yards. He was therefore understandably confused when new coach Josh McDaniels started to publicly court the New England Patriots' backup Matt Cassel.

Cutler values loyalty and keeps his circle of friends and business associates close, generally sticking with people from his childhood and his days at Vanderbilt. And so, after feeling betrayed by Denver, he asked to be let out. The Broncos obliged in 2009 and sent him to Chicago for the Bears' quarterback Kyle Orton and three draft picks, including two first-rounders.

Cutler didn't let his favorite childhood team down — after three years with Chicago, he holds the Bears' highest career quarterback rating (82.9) and passing yards per game average (225.8); he was also

the first to post back-to-back 3,000-yard and 20+ touchdown seasons, was the fastest to throw for 3,000 yards (13 games), and he holds the franchise records for single-season attempts (555) and completions (336).

Unfortunately for Cutler, his enduring image in a Bears uniform has been of him standing on the sidelines following the 2010 NFC Championship game against the Bears' archrival Green Bay Packers. Poised to go to the Super Bowl, Cutler suffered a knee injury and couldn't finish the game, which the Bears lost. He stood on the sidelines, looking as if he had quit, and he was torn apart by both the media and fellow NFL players.

IN THE HUDDLE

Cutler threw for a touchdown on his first career postseason attempt, and he's the second player in NFL history (after Otto Graham in 1955) with two passing and two rushing touchdowns in a playoff game (a 35–24 win over Seattle in January 2011).

Coach Lovie Smith and team leader Brian Urlacher defended their quarterback, and Cutler could have helped the situation by explaining to the media that planting his leg and throwing the ball would have been impossible with the MCL tear

he sustained, but he simply didn't say a word about it.

There's no question, however, that the team's fortunes ride on Cutler's arm. Case in point: in 2011, the Bears were on a five-game winning streak and were poised for a playoff run when Cutler broke his thumb. Without him, the Bears lost their next five games and missed the postseason.

Cutler is not one to gloat about how much his team needs him, which is similar to his stand on turning down endorsements until the Bears win the Super Bowl. He also doesn't advertise all the charity work he quietly does for underprivileged children and kids with diabetes. But, as private as Cutler is, he has found his way into celebrity gossip magazines thanks to his on-again/off-again relationship with reality star Kristin Cavallari, who he's now engaged to, with a new baby boy to boot.

With the addition to his family and the Bears' acquisition of receiver and former teammate Brandon Marshall, 2012 could be a big year for Cutler. And if he can deliver a long-awaited second Super Bowl to Chicago, the man from Santa Claus won't need to be jolly, and he will definitely be more popular than Christmas.

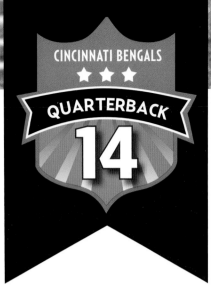

ANDY DALTON

Prior to 2011, the Bengals were becoming known for living up to their "Bungles" nickname, and after spending the previous year indulging aging receivers and all-world showboats Chad Ochocinco and Terrell Owens, the team let them both go for the 2011 season, which prompted their best player, quarterback Carson Palmer, to say he would never suit up for Cincinnati again. Coming off a 4–12 season and with all their marquee names leaving town, 2011 for the Bengals looked like it was going to be another year at the bottom of the NFL barrel. But, along came a quiet redheaded kid from Texas Christian University (TCU) to help steady the ship and breathe hope into the franchise.

Quarterback Andy Dalton entered the league as the Bengals' second-round pick in 2011, and he had nowhere near the hype or headlines surrounding young quarterbacks Cam Newton and Tim Tebow. Dalton was the fifth quarterback taken in the draft and few were predicting he would be a Cincinnati savior, even after his stellar career at TCU.

Dalton had been underestimated before; in high school he didn't start at quarterback until his senior season, but he led his Katy High School team to the Texas state finals that year, throwing for 2,877 yards and 42 touchdowns.

In his freshman year at TCU, Dalton went a modest 8–5, but followed that up with an 11–2 season as a sophomore. As a junior and senior he led the Horned Frogs to national prominence with back-to-back undefeated regular seasons and Mountain West Conference titles. In his final college game he was the Offensive MVP in a 21–19 Rose Bowl victory over Wisconsin. TCU finished the year 13–0 and ranked second in the country.

Dalton's record over four years was 42–7, which surpassed NFL Hall of Famer Sammy Baugh for the most victories in school history. Dalton also set marks in just about

CAREER HIGHLIGHTS
- Rose Bowl Offensive MVP (2010)
- Two-time Mountain West Conference Offensive Player of the Year (2009, 2010)
- Pro Bowl alternate (2011)

every quarterback category at TCU, including passing yards, completions, completion percentage and touchdown passes.

Respect still didn't follow. Dalton was ninth in Heisman voting during his senior season and scouts questioned his arm strength. Cincinnati coach Marvin Lewis, however, knew he had found a winner at the 2011 draft: "We went through quite a process looking at all the quarterbacks [in the draft], and we were drawn to Andy because he's a guy we believe can come in and contribute immediately if need be. He's mature enough and ready to handle it. What he accomplished at TCU goes without saying."

Lewis proved to be prescient; Dalton did contribute immediately, and he wasn't fazed by running an NFL offense. In October 2011 he was named Offensive Rookie of the Month after throwing for 909 yards and six touchdowns, with the Bengals going 4–0. And, perhaps more importantly, Dalton gave the

front office the confidence to trade Palmer, sending him to the Oakland Raiders for a first-round pick and a conditional second-round pick.

IN THE HUDDLE
Dalton holds the Texas Christian University career records for wins (42), touchdown passes (71), passing yards (10,314), pass attempts (1,317), completions (812) and completion percentage (61.6).

The Bengals finished the 2011 season 9–7 (only their third winning season in the last 20 years), with Dalton throwing for 3,398 yards and 20 touchdowns to join the ranks of Newton and the Indianapolis Colts' Peyton Manning as only the third rookie quarterback with over 3,000 yards and 20 TDs.

If it weren't for Newton's ridiculous statistics (the best a rookie quarterback in the NFL has ever had), Dalton likely would have claimed Offensive Rookie of the Year in 2011. He did earn something

Newton didn't, though — a playoff berth.

The Bengals bowed out to the Houston Texans in the first round, but Dalton had undoubtedly gained the faith of the Bengals' brain trust and fan base, as well as a spot in the Pro Bowl (as an alternate). Further, with his nomination to be included on the All-Star Game roster, Dalton became just the fourth quarterback drafted in the second round in the past 27 years to make the team. Brett Favre, Drew Brees and former Bengal Boomer Esiason are the others — pretty heady company.

Joining Dalton in Hawaii for the Pro Bowl was fellow Bengals first-year sensation A.J. Green, who was named a starter at wide receiver. The Bengals certainly didn't "bungle" the 2011 draft. They're now the first team to ever produce a rookie 3,000-yard passer and a rookie 1,000-yard receiver, and with the two picks they acquired from Oakland for Palmer, the Bengals are poised to become a deep young squad in the years to come.

NEW YORK GIANTS

★ ★ ★

QUARTERBACK

10

ELI MANNING

It's rough being a younger brother, and between the hand-me-down clothes and the noogies, it's even tougher when your name is Elisha. But with his laid-back demeanor and easy calm, Eli Manning has managed to take it all in stride, even when his big brother, Peyton, became a four-time NFL MVP and eventual first-ballot Hall of Famer.

It's this serenity that has allowed Manning to survive in the media cauldron of the Big Apple as quarterback for the New York Giants. His calm assuredness was on duty just prior to the 2011 season after he was asked during a radio interview if he considered himself "in Tom Brady's class." Manning responded confidently, "Yeah, I consider myself in that class," and the quote took on a life of its own, with many ridiculing Manning for putting himself among such highly regarded company. He shrugged and went about his business, just as he had since he followed Peyton into the quarterback role at Isidore Newman High School in New Orleans, where the boys grew up after their father Archie played quarterback for the Saints.

"[Eli is] as laid-back and easygoing as you'll see… He doesn't get rattled," says Frank Gendusa, who coached the Manning boys at Isidore Newman.

All-District, All-State and All-American, Manning chose

CAREER HIGHLIGHTS

- Two-time Super Bowl champion (XLII, XLVI)

- Two-time Super Bowl MVP (XLII, XLVI)

- Two-time Pro Bowl selection (2008, 2011)

- Has the longest active streak of games started among quarterbacks (130, including playoffs), which surpasses Peyton Manning, who missed the 2011 season (the streak is the most by a Giants quarterback and the sixth-longest for the position in NFL history) to attend the University of Mississippi, where his father was a legend and his eldest brother Cooper had been a receiver before a congenital narrowing of the spine cut his football career short. Manning left Ole Miss with 47 game, season and career records and a wheelbarrow full of awards before being picked first overall by the San Diego Chargers in 2004. San Diego and New York then made a draft-day trade, sending Eli to the Giants for quarterback Philip Rivers and three draft picks.

Despite regularly throwing for over 3,000 yards and 20 touchdowns a season, Manning played in Peyton's shadow for three years — until one of the most spectacular plays in Super Bowl history.

IN THE HUDDLE

Manning holds the NFL record for most fourth-quarter touchdown passes in a season (15), the record for most road playoff wins by a quarterback (5) and the most consecutive passes completed to open a Super Bowl (9).

No one gave the 2007 Giants much of a chance for the championship. Sure, they had won three playoff games on the road, but they were 12-point underdogs against the New England Patriots and the unflappable Tom Brady. Manning, however, matched Brady punch for punch, and late in the fourth quarter the Patriots were up only 14–10. With less than three minutes remaining, Manning marched the Giants down the field from their own 17-yard line. This drive included what NFL Films' Steve Sabol called "the greatest play the Super Bowl has ever produced." Manning looked like he was going to be sacked by three Patriots, but he escaped and threw the ball to David Tyree, who made a leaping one-handed grab and pinned the ball to his helmet while he was being hit. Four plays later, Manning found Plaxico Burress in the end zone for the winning points in a 17–14 victory that ended the Patriots' dream of a perfect season and earned Manning the Super Bowl MVP award.

In 2011, Manning backed up his preseason claim against Brady with a career-best 4,933 yards, the sixth-highest total in NFL history. He also set a record for fourth-quarter touchdowns in a season (15) and led the Giants to the playoffs by winning three of their last four games, which included two against their archrival, the Dallas Cowboys.

The momentum carried over into the postseason. After beating the Atlanta Falcons, the Giants traveled to Green Bay to take on the 15–1 Packers; Manning and his team left town with a 37–20 victory and a trip to the NFC Championship against the resurgent San Francisco 49ers.

It was here that Manning was hit 20 times and sacked six, but somehow still managed to lead the Giants to a gutsy 20–17 overtime victory. The win set up a rematch with the New England Patriots four years after one of the biggest upsets in Super Bowl history. Fans and advertisers were thrilled, and a sense of déjà vu took over.

Once again it came down to the fourth quarter and another spectacular catch, this time a sideline tightrope-walk by Mario Manningham after Manning placed the ball perfectly between two defenders. Seven plays later, the Patriots allowed Ahmad Bradshaw to score so they would have more time on the clock, but Brady couldn't replicate his counterpart's heroics, and when his last-second Hail Mary fell short, Manning began celebrations of both his second Super Bowl victory and his second MVP award.

After defeating Brady twice in four years, Manning is undoubtedly considered elite and has earned some serious bragging rights — not that he cares.

DENVER BRONCOS
★ ★ ★
QUARTERBACK
18

PEYTON MANNING

For a man who didn't play a down during the 2011 season, Peyton Manning's shadow loomed large over the Indianapolis Colts and the NFL.

The Colts went from a perennial contender with an average of 10.8 victories a year in the Manning era (1998 to 2010) to having only two wins in 2011, which prompted writer Thomas George to name Manning the league's MVP. Although it was meant to stir up controversy and sell copies of the first issue of *NFL Magazine,* George had a point: the precipitous drop in the team's fortunes demonstrated just how valuable Manning is to the Colts. Management also proved it by giving him a five-year, $90 million contract after the 2010 season, just prior to the cervical fusion surgery in his neck that spelled an end to his 2011 season.

The win average of 10.8 includes the three-victory season of 1998 when Manning, the first overall pick, was at the helm of an NFL team only a year after he became the University of Tennessee's all-time leading passer. Manning wasn't to blame for the 3–13 season. The Colts lost five games in which they had double-digit leads, but Manning still set five NFL rookie records, including most touchdown passes.

The following season, the Colts found a way to hold their leads and set an NFL record with a 10-win turnaround to finish 13–3, winning

- University of Tennessee's all-time leading passer with 11,201 yards, 863 completions and 89 touchdowns
- Holds 42 NCAA, SEC and Tennessee records, including 33 Tennessee single-game, season and career records
- Is the only NFL player with over 40,000 passing yards (42,322) and over 300 passing touchdowns (314) in a decade (2000–09); his 3,579 completions and 115 starting wins also rank as the most in a single decade
- Was the MVP in the Colts' 29–17 victory over the Chicago Bears in Super Bowl XLI
- Winner of the Walter Payton NFL Man of the Year Award, the Henry P. Iba Citizen Athlete Award, USA Weekend's Most Caring Athlete Award, the Youthlinks Indiana National Pathfinder Award and the Byron "Whizzer" White Humanitarian Award

11 of their final 12 games with Manning throwing for 4,135 yards and being named to his first All-Pro and Pro Bowl teams.

Going forward, all Manning did was improve. He earned NFL MVP honors in 2003, 2004, 2008 and 2009, becoming the only player in NFL history to win this accolade four times. He's made 11 Pro Bowl appearances and has been named to the All-Pro First Team five times, including three consecutive seasons from 2003–05.

IN THE HUDDLE
Manning's four NFL MVP Awards (in 2003, 2004, 2008 and 2009) total the most earned by any player in the history of the league.

Manning also holds NFL records for consecutive seasons with over 4,000 yards passing (6) and the most total seasons with 4,000 or more yards passing in a career (11). He's the Colts' all-time leader in career wins (141), career passing yards (54,828), pass attempts (7,210), pass completions (4,682) and passing touchdowns (399).

Some, however, consider February 4, 2007, to be Manning's finest hour. On this day, he led Indianapolis to a 29–17 victory over the Chicago Bears in Super Bowl XLI and was named the game's MVP. He brought the Colts back to the big dance three years later, but the New Orleans Saints prevailed 31–17 in Super Bowl XLIV.

If there's a knock on Manning — one of the best players in NFL history — it's that he only has one Super Bowl victory, but pointing that out is like complaining that the Colosseum in Rome hasn't stood the test of time. Manning has been a gladiator over the course of his career, playing in 227 consecutive games (including playoffs) before his neck surgery in 2011. He's also been the top ambassador for America's most popular league; according to Forbes, he makes more than twice as much off the field as any other NFL player, thanks to a squeaky-clean image and a sense of humor that has earned him hosting duties on *Saturday Night Live*.

Manning is taken seriously as well, and he's known as one of the most cerebral, intense players in the league, demanding perfection from himself and his teammates. In recognition of these traits, he has won numerous humanitarian awards, including the Walter Payton NFL Man of the Year Award.

So how could the Colts let him walk away? With a $28 million bonus due to Manning, and unsure of how he'd rebound from neck surgery, the club made the difficult decision to cut Manning loose. The Colts then picked Stanford's Andrew Luck with the first overall pick in the draft to replace Manning.

Leaving the Colts with the same class he always conducted himself with in Indianapolis, Manning stood alongside owner Jim Irsay when the announcement was made and emotionally thanked the city and organization, saying goodbye to the only professional home he'd ever known.

A high-profile courtship by the lion's share of the league ensued, and speculation was rife over where Manning would land. He took many by surprise when he chose to go to the Denver Broncos, ending the Tim Tebow era and immediately making the Broncos a contender.

Tebow was a scrapper who brought the spotlight to Denver in 2011, Manning is a thoroughbred who, if healthy, will keep it shining brightly there, and probably deeper into the postseason.

CAROLINA PANTHERS
★ ★ ★

QUARTERBACK
1

CAM
NEWTON

For a man with such sublime football talent, Cam Newton sure has a knack for getting overshadowed. The Carolina Panthers quarterback has twice taken a backseat to Tim Tebow and scandal has followed him throughout his career.

After graduating from Westlake High School in Atlanta, Georgia, Newton had more than 40 scholarship offers, but most schools wanted him to be a tight end. Newton ended up choosing the University of Florida — despite the fact that Tebow was already an established quarterback there — because he thought their offensive system suited him and he would eventually get a chance to win the quarterback job.

Newton's career in Florida turned out to be pretty quiet. As a freshman in 2007, he got into five games, threw for a total of 40 yards and ran for 103, and in his first game as a sophomore, he injured his ankle and sat out the season as a medical redshirt. That year, however, he was arrested for stealing a laptop, and even though the charges were dropped after he agreed to a diversion program, the incident spelled the end of his time with Florida.

In January 2009, Newton transferred to Blinn College in Brenham, Texas, and he led the Buccaneers to the national junior college championship in his lone season there. This earned him the attention of the Division I schools for a second time. Spoiled for choice, he decided on Auburn University.

Unbeknownst to Newton at the time, his father Cecil had approached Mississippi State University and offered his son's services for a six-figure payment. When the allegations came to light, Newton was briefly suspended and then quickly reinstated after the NCAA found no wrongdoing on the part of Newton or Auburn.

Throughout the scandal, Newton had one of the best seasons a college quarterback has ever had, breaking a slew of school and conference records, winning every major individual trophy — including the Heisman — and leading Auburn to its first national title since 1957.

IN THE HUDDLE

Newton's father Cecil tried out for the Dallas Cowboys and the Buffalo Bills, and older brother Cecil Jr. has been on the roster of the Baltimore Ravens and the Packers as a center/guard.

Newton had another year of eligibility on the college scene, but with nothing left to prove, the Panthers snapped him up with the number one pick after he declared for the 2010 NFL draft. Newton quickly got to work. In his first game he threw for 422 yards (breaking Peyton Manning's record for an NFL debut), and he followed that up with a 432-yard game in a narrow 23–20 loss to the defending Super Bowl–champion Green Bay Packers. This was a feat that set the mark for most yards in a game by a rookie quarterback, and it was also the highest total after two career starts. Newton cruised from there, setting the record for rushing touchdowns by a quarterback with 14, becoming the first rookie to have over 4,000 yards passing and going down in history as the first quarterback to ever have over 4,000 yards passing and 500 yards rushing in a season.

Any other year, Newton probably would have been the biggest story in the league, but Packers quarterback Aaron Rodgers was having one of the greatest years in NFL history, and Tebow, now starting for the Denver Broncos as a rookie, was stealing the spotlight with his fourth-quarter comebacks and ascension to pop-culture fame. It also didn't help that the Panthers finished the season out of the playoffs with a 6–10 record.

To be fair, Newton had joined one of the weaker teams in the league, but when he was asked how it felt to put up such spectacular numbers as his team piled up losses, he responded: "What happens when you take a lion out of the safari and try to take him to your place of residence and make him a house pet? It ain't going to happen. That's the type of person that I am. I'm that lion. The house that I'm in is somewhat of a tarnished house where losing is accepted. But I'm trying to change that, whether I'm going to have to turn that house into a safari, or I'm just going to have to get out of that house. I'm not saying I'm trying to leave this place. I'm just trying to get everybody on my level."

It's an audacious statement from a player in his first season, but if Newton can let his play on the field do the talking and lead the Panthers back to the Super Bowl, he might end up as one of the best quarterbacks of his generation.

CAREER HIGHLIGHTS

- Heisman Trophy winner (2010)
- First quarterback in NFL history to pass for more than 400 yards in first career start
- First quarterback in NFL history to pass for more than 400 yards in first two career starts
- First rookie in NFL history to pass for more than 400 yards in back-to-back games
- Fastest player to throw for 1,000 yards
- First player in NFL history with at least five rushing touchdowns and five passing touchdowns in his first five games
- First rookie in NFL history to throw for 10 touchdowns and run for 10 touchdowns in a season
- First rookie quarterback to throw for 4,000 yards in a season
- First quarterback to throw for 4,000 yards (4,051) and rush for 500 yards (706) in a single season
- Most rushing touchdowns in single season by a quarterback (14)
- Offensive Rookie of the Year (2011)
- Pro Bowl selection (2011)

PHILIP RIVERS

The San Diego Chargers' Philip Rivers is the Kevin Bacon of NFL quarterbacks — there are few degrees of separation between him and the league's other elite passers. Rivers was essentially swapped for Eli Manning on draft day when Manning refused to sign with San Diego, who had the first overall pick. Rivers was also drafted fourth by the New York Giants in 2004, which was seven spots ahead of the Pittsburgh Steelers' Ben Roethlisberger at

11. Once in San Diego, Rivers ended up wresting the starting job from Drew Brees, who's now breaking records with the New Orleans Saints.

Manning, Roethlisberger and Brees, however, have all been the MVP in Super Bowl victories, and until Rivers is able to join that exclusive club, he will always come up short in ultimate quarterback comparisons.

Rivers has the tools to get there. He's the son of a football

coach, he grew up with the game and was always poised and confident beyond his years. He was the starting quarterback and occasional free safety at Athens High, in Alabama, where his dad coached. As a senior he was voted the state's player of the year, but he wasn't recruited as a quarterback by any marquee schools because he had an unusual delivery. North Carolina State University assistant coach Joe Pate had no reservations about Rivers' ability, though: "I concentrated more on the results of his throws, and I realized he was the best quarterback that I'd ever recruited."

N.C. State quarterbacks coach Norm Chow (who has worked with legends Steve Young, Jim McMahon and Ty Detmer) was concerned about Rivers' delivery, so he asked friend and then-Seahawks coach Mike Holmgren for some input. "Does he throw strong and accurately?" asked Holmgren. "If so, leave him alone."

It was wise advice, as Rivers was the undisputed leader of the offense from his first season in North Carolina, earning the respect of his teammates and putting N.C. State on the football map for the first time in decades. The team had a winning record

in each of Rivers' four seasons, ending three with a victory in a bowl game, and in Rivers' senior year, he was named ACC Athlete of the Year and Senior Bowl MVP.

IN THE HUDDLE
Since Rivers became a starter in his junior year of high school, he's never had a losing record at any level.

Despite his collegiate success and high draft spot, when Rivers reached the NFL he sat on the bench for two seasons—but he didn't pout about it. Instead, he used that time to learn from veterans Brees and Doug Flutie, and when he became the starter in 2006, the Chargers had enough confidence in Rivers to let Brees go.

In his six seasons as a starter Rivers has led the Chargers to four AFC West titles and three playoff wins, and has thrown for over 4,000 yards in each of his last four seasons, becoming just the third quarterback in NFL history to do so.

Entering the 2011 season, Rivers was the Chargers' all-time leader for career completion percentage (.637) and passer rating (97.2), which was the second-highest rating in NFL history. This was also the year in which many pundits predicted the Chargers would end their season in Super Bowl XLVI, with Rivers as a strong candidate to be NFL MVP. The team, however, couldn't recover from some narrow losses and critical errors early in the schedule, and they finished 8–8 and out of the AFC playoff picture.

Rivers can take some solace in being named to his fourth Pro Bowl after a strong second half, and following his record-breaking season, he still belongs among the best of the best — not that Rivers invites comparison.

"One thing I've learned is that all the quarterbacks in this league can throw," says Rivers. "It's the guys who can handle a little adversity — handle the *NFL Primetime* guys analyzing them or the fans saying things — that last. If you let [critics] beat you up, it'll run you out of the league. You can't worry about it. And besides, the only thing that really matters is where you finish."

CAREER HIGHLIGHTS
- ACC Athlete of the Year (2004)
- Senior Bowl MVP (2004)
- NFL Alumni Quarterback of the Year (2010)
- San Diego Chargers 50th Anniversary Team
- Four-time Pro Bowl selection (2006, 2009, 2010, 2011)

BEN ROETHLISBERGER

The 1983 draft is regarded as the deepest — as far as quarterbacks are concerned — in NFL history, with future Hall of Famers John Elway, Jim Kelly and Dan Marino all taken in the first round. The class of 2004, however, is giving these men a run for their money, thanks to the New York Giants' Eli Manning, the San Diego Chargers' Philip Rivers and the Pittsburgh Steelers' Ben Roethlisberger.

IN THE HUDDLE

Roethlisberger's 13 straight victories in his first season set an NFL record for the most games won by a rookie in league history. His 51 wins in his first five seasons were the most by any quarterback in the history of the NFL, and at age 23, Roethlisberger became the youngest quarterback to ever win the Super Bowl.

Born in Lima and raised in Findlay, Ohio, Roethlisberger captained three sports at his high school, but he didn't get to play the quarterback position until his senior year, when his coach's son graduated. Roethlisberger stepped easily into the role and won the Ohio Offensive Player of the Year award, as well as set state records with 4,041 yards and 54 touchdowns.

Later, at Miami University (Ohio), Roethlisberger set 21 school records, including career completions (854), passing yards (10,829) and touchdown passes (84), and he was a three-time All-Mid-American Conference selection and three-time team MVP. In 2007, the RedHawks retired his number, which was the first to be retired in 30 years and only the third to be honored in the team's history.

Roethlisberger left Miami University after his junior year and was drafted 11th overall by the Steelers. He first saw NFL action in the second game of his rookie season, and he promptly won 13 straight games and set rookie records for wins, passer rating (98.1) and completion percentage (66.4).

After finishing 15–1 and reaching the AFC Championship in 2004, the Steelers' had to rally in 2005, as they needed to win their last four games in order to reach the playoffs as a wild-card entry. Roethlisberger, who had

injuries to his thumb and knee, led Pittsburgh to two road victories to reach the AFC Championship for the second time.

On the road against the Indianapolis Colts, it looked like the Steelers' 2005 season had come to an end when the Colts' Nick Harper picked up a fumble with less than two minutes left. Headed for what looked like a sure touchdown and a trip to the Super Bowl, Harper ran into the last man between him and the end zone — the 6-foot-4, 240-pound Roethlisberger, who brought Harper down with one arm and secured the win for the Steelers.

Roethlisberger's Super Bowl XL performance was equally memorable, but for one of the ugliest stat lines in history — 9 completions for 123 yards, no touchdowns and 2 interceptions. The Steelers ended up winning 21–10 over the Seattle Seahawks, which made Roethlisberger both the youngest quarterback and the lowest-rated passer to ever win the Super Bowl.

The Steelers reached the Super Bowl again in 2008, and Roethlisberger almost matched his passing total from Super Bowl XL … on the first two

drives. Trailing 23–20 against the Arizona Cardinals and with just over two minutes left in the game, Roethlisberger took the Steelers 88 yards on 8 plays, throwing an inch-perfect pass to Santonio Holmes in the corner of the end zone with 35 seconds left to win the game.

Roethlisberger's life, however, hasn't been quite as perfect. After a golf tournament in Lake Tahoe in 2008, he was accused of sexual assault by a hotel employee. The charges were eventually dropped, but Roethlisberger was arrested a second time in 2010 after an alleged encounter with a college student in Georgia. Prosecutors didn't pursue the case but NFL commissioner Roger Goodell suspended Roethlisberger for six games under the league's personal-conduct policy. Roethlisberger convinced Goodell he understood the gravity of his

actions and was going to turn his life around, so his suspension was later reduced to four games.

Nevertheless, no can deny Roethlisberger's talent. "Big Ben" has been to three Super Bowl, owns 31 franchise records — including single-season records for passing yards (4,328), completions (337), passer rating (104.1) and touchdowns (32) — broke Terry Bradshaw's team record for career completions (2,025) in 2011 and finished the year with 2,090.

"The respect we have for Ben is that we don't look at him as a diva quarterback," says New York Jets linebacker Bart Scott. "We look at him as a football player. In this league, especially now, quarterbacks are treated pretty much like it's flag football. But he's one that's willing to take the hits and look down the barrel of a gun for his team."

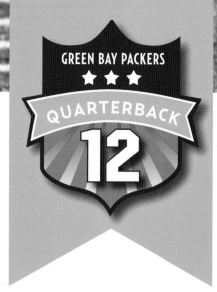

AARON RODGERS

In a year when two quarterbacks (Tom Brady and Drew Brees) surpassed Dan Marino's 27-year-old single-season passing record of 5,084 yards, it was likely assumed that they would be the front-runners in the NFL's MVP voting. It was not to be — in 2011, the honor went to the Green Bay Packers' quarterback Aaron Rodgers.

Before the 2011 season, Rodgers was the all-time leader in career quarterback rating (98.4), and that year, he also set the single-season record with 122.5, upping his career rating to 104.1. Rodgers threw for 45 touchdowns and only 6 interceptions, and with 4,643 yards passing he could have thrown for over 5,000 yards had the Packers not strategically rested him for the final game of the regular season.

Rodgers' early talents were honed at Pleasant Valley High School in Chico, California, where the skinny senior with the rocket arm and size-14 feet had only one college coach to come to his house — by walking across the street — to recruit him. Neighbor Craig Rigsbee coached at Butte College, and in Rodgers' single season there, he led the team to a 10–1 record. His talent caught the eye of Jeff Tedford, the head coach at the University of California, Berkeley,

and Rodgers spent two seasons becoming the highest rated passer in school history before declaring for the NFL draft a year early and getting picked by the Packers with the 24th overall selection in 2005.

At that point, Green Bay star Brett Favre had played every game for 16 seasons, won the MVP award three times and set NFL career records for completions, yards and touchdowns. Thus, Rodgers threw all of 59 passes in his first three seasons. Choosing not to complain about the lack of playing time or opportunity, he focused on learning from his future Hall-of-Fame teammate.

The tables turned before the 2008 season when the Packers pondered a quarterback switch and Favre publicly flirted with other teams. The result was a messy divorce that ended up with Rodgers taking the reins in 2008. Favre, however, refused to go away and he played a season with the New York Jets before joining the Minnesota Vikings — the Packers' NFC North rival.

Rodgers stayed away from the controversy and instead became the first quarterback to throw for over 4,000 yards in each of his first two full seasons. He has only fallen short of that mark once (by 78 yards in 2010), when he missed a game and a half with a concussion.

In 2010, the Packers made the playoffs on the last day of the season as the wild-card entry. From there, they went on to beat the top-three seeds in the NFC to reach Super Bowl XLV against the Pittsburgh Steelers. Rodgers became the fourth quarterback in history to throw for over 300 yards and 3 touchdowns in a Super Bowl, as he led the Packers to the title, earning himself the MVP award in the process.

The off-season did nothing to cool down the Packers (they lost only one game the entire calendar

year), and on the first day of 2012, in the last game of the 2011 regular season, Rodgers took a rest while backup Matt Flynn threw for 480 yards and 6 touchdowns in a 45–41 win over the Detroit Lions, both of which were records that broke franchise single-game marks.

Unfortunately, that single day off — followed by the bye week the Packers had earned with the best record in the league — might have hurt Rodgers. In the divisional playoff against the New York Giants, Rodgers was sacked four times and threw for only 264 yards with a quarterback rating of 78.5 in a 37–20 loss.

IN THE HUDDLE
Rodgers is the first quarterback in NFL history with at least three touchdown passes in each of his first three playoff starts, and with ratings of 121.4, 122.5 and 136.8 in those games he became the first quarterback to go over 120 in his first three playoff appearances.

No matter — Rodgers and the Packers had a near-perfect year in 2011, and at 28 years old, Rodgers has a lot of football left in him, as well as the drive and temperament to get his team back to the top.

Now that Wisconsin's state assembly has named December 12, 2012 Aaron Rodgers Day, it looks like No. 12 is firmly ensconced as Wisconsin's favorite adopted son. He has the number-one-selling jersey in the NFL, was named the league's most marketable player, and in November 2011 was named third in an American poll of favorability (behind Jesus and Abraham Lincoln, but placed in front of George Washington, Martin Luther King, Gandhi, Mother Teresa and Santa Claus).

Rodgers is ahead of some lofty company, fictional or otherwise, and armed with his impressive numbers and talent, he should be ready to take on 2012.

CAREER HIGHLIGHTS
- NFL MVP (2011)
- Associated Press Male Athlete of the Year (2011)
- Super Bowl XLV MVP
- Two-time Pro Bowl selection (2009, 2011)
- All-Pro (2011)
- Set the single-season quarterback rating record with 122.5 in 2011

DALLAS COWBOYS
★ ★ ★
QUARTERBACK
9

TONY ROMO

The quarterback of the Dallas Cowboys is one of the most romantic positions in all of sports, evoking images of a square-jawed hero leading "America's Team" to the championship with a star on his helmet and a starlet on his arm. However, being put on that pedestal also invites scrutiny.

In some ways, Tony Romo has lived up to the image, embracing the celebrity lifestyle and dating famous women, but he wasn't born into it. Romo came from humble roots and, seemingly out of nowhere, worked his way to the top.

At Burlington High School in Wisconsin, Romo was a multisport athlete and was named to the All-State football team, but he wasn't a blue-chip prospect and ended up one tier below the big boys with a partial scholarship to Eastern Illinois University in Division I-AA. In four years at the school, he was named the Ohio Valley Conference Player of the Year three times, won the Walter Payton Award as the best player in Division I-AA and had his number retired, which was the first time the school had bestowed that honor on a player.

Apparently scouts missed the ceremony; Romo wasn't drafted and instead signed with the Cowboys as a free agent in 2003. He then spent three seasons on the sidelines as a third-string quarterback who had little indication from the team that he would ever get a chance to play, let alone become a star. Finally, in 2006, he went in for Drew Bledsoe and started to build his resume.

In 2007, his first full season as a starter, Romo led the Cowboys to 13 wins, tying the franchise record for victories in a season and setting the single-season club marks for touchdown passes (36), completions (335), yardage (4,211) and 300-yard games (7).

CAREER HIGHLIGHTS

- Three-time Ohio Valley Conference Player of the Year (2000, 2001, 2002)

- Three-time Division I-AA All-American (2000, 2001, 2002)

- Walter Payton Award winner as the top player in Division I-AA (2002)

- Three-time Pro Bowl Selection (2006, 2007, 2009)

- Set a Cowboys record for consecutive games with a touchdown pass with 17 straight between 2006 and 2007, and broke the record with 18 in 2009 and 2010

Befitting the high-profile nature of the team, he quickly rose to prominence with 6 of his first 11 starts being nationally televised. He also made headlines by dating singer and reality star Jessica Simpson and by vacationing with her in Mexico a week before a playoff game against the New York Giants. The criticism was withering after the Cowboys lost and were eliminated.

IN THE HUDDLE

In 2011, Romo passed Steve Young for the second-highest career passer rating in NFL history (96.9), which was behind only Aaron Rodgers of the Green Bay Packers.

Romo's football seasons tend to slow down as the year wears on and falter when it matters most. His record in the months of December and January was 10–16, his playoff record was 1–3, and the enduring memory of his playoff career, apart from the paparazzi pictures with

Simpson in Mexico, is of when in 2007 he bobbled the hold on a short field goal at the end of a game that was lost 21–20 to the Seattle Seahawks.

Questions about his commitment, however, should have been answered in September 2011, when he broke a rib and punctured his lung in the first half against the San Francisco 49ers, returned to the field after a painkiller injection at halftime and rallied the team to win in overtime. Romo also had the highest quarterback rating of his career in 2011, surpassing 100 for the first time (102.5), while passing for over 4,000 yards for the third time in his career. His numbers weren't quite enough for the 8–8 Cowboys, though, and Dallas missed the playoffs by going 1–4 to end the year, including two losses to the Giants, one of which was on the final day of the season.

When the only goal is the Super Bowl, 2011 was another lost season for America's Team. After Indianapolis released Peyton Manning, Dallas

fans beseeched the team to sign him, whatever the cost, reasoning that Romo would never get them over the hump. Dallas fans were sure the four-time MVP and Super Bowl winner was the answer to their championship prayers.

But Dallas management chose not to pursue Manning, and owner Jerry Jones publicly stated that the team wouldn't choose a quarterback in the first round of the 2012 draft.

The team has assured Romo is their quarterback now, and possibly for the future. Keeping with the faith that his teammates share, the club has discussed a contract extension with Romo that would keep him in Dallas beyond 2014. The Cowboys' star tight end, Jason Witten, a favorite passing target of Romo's, says he wouldn't trade Romo for Manning, or for anyone else. "[Romo] is easygoing and laid back. [But people ask] does he have enough to take the team. I mean, does he have that 'Peyton Manning' attitude where the team's under his arms? He's got that."

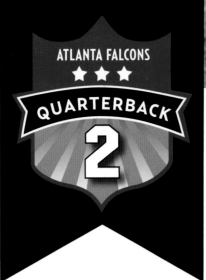

MATT RYAN

Coming into the NFL in 2008 as a rookie quarterback for the Atlanta Falcons, Matt Ryan was immediately placed on one of the hottest seats in football — he had the unenviable task of becoming the face of the franchise only one year after fan-favorite Michael Vick's sudden departure.

Vick was one of the league's most talented and dynamic quarterbacks, but in 2007 he was arrested and imprisoned for his part in a dogfighting ring. The Falcons released him, but a serious blow had been dealt to the franchise and fans were looking for a savior.

Ryan grew up in Pennsylvania and attended William Penn Charter School in Philadelphia, where he was the senior captain of the baseball, basketball and football teams and threw for more than 1,300 yards and 15 touchdowns to earn a scholarship to Boston College. While in Boston, Ryan broke many of Doug Flutie's school records, including single-season passing yards (4,507), career completions (807) and games with 400-plus yards passing (5). He was also christened "Matty Ice" for his poise under pressure, was the 2007 ACC Player of the Year and was the winner of the Manning Award as the nation's top quarterback (2007). However, it might have been a third 2007 trophy, the Johnny Unitas Golden Arm Award, that

really caught the attention of the Falcons. At the time, an award based on athletic performance as well as character, leadership and academic performance (and that was given to a senior quarterback) was probably even more important to Atlanta than the Heisman.

IN THE HUDDLE

Ryan was the first rookie quarterback in Falcons history to win 11 games. He was the first rookie quarterback (along with Joe Flacco) to start all 16 games and lead his team to the playoffs.

With Joey Harrington quarterbacking the Falcons in 2007 immediately following Vick's departure, the team went 4–12, which only added to the pressure Ryan felt after the team picked him third overall in 2008. Expectations were high, but he lived up to them, and the first pass of his NFL career was a 65-yard touchdown pass to Michael Jenkins. By the end of the year, Ryan won the Offensive Rookie of the Year award throwing for 3,440 yards and 17 touchdowns.

Ryan started each of his 16 games in 2008, the Falcons had an 11–5 record and the team made the playoffs for the first time since 2004. In the opening round, the Falcons faced the Arizona Cardinals and veteran quarterback Kurt Warner;

Ryan almost matched him shot-for-shot, but the Falcons eventually fell 30–24.

In 2009, Ryan hurt his foot in a game against the Tampa Bay Buccaneers in Week 12. He missed his next two games, which were both losses. The team ended the season with a 9–7 record but missed the playoffs. Those post-injury games were the only ones Ryan has missed in his career, and it was the only season Atlanta didn't make the playoffs since their new star quarterback joined the team.

Ryan and the Falcons came back strong in 2010, earning a first-round bye after a 13–3 season in which he set the franchise mark with 357 completions and was named to his first Pro Bowl. Everything ended on a sour note, however, as the Falcons fell 48–21 to the eventual Super Bowl champion, the Green Bay Packers.

In 2011, Ryan threw for a franchise-record 4,177 yards and, leapfrogging Vick, became the team's second all-time leader in passing after only four seasons. This year, Ryan and Vick also had their first showdown when the Philadelphia Eagles visited the Georgia Dome in September. The Eagles were leading 24–21 in the third quarter, but Vick was knocked out of the game with a concussion. From there, Ryan rallied his troops, and the Falcons had two touchdowns in the fourth quarter to win 35–31.

The game lifted Ryan to new heights in the eyes of the Falcons faithful, and the come-from-behind victory might have been the most satisfying of the team's 10 wins that season. That same magic couldn't be conjured in the playoffs, though, and once again Atlanta bowed out in the first round to the eventual Super Bowl champions, this time the New York Giants.

The loss to the Giants was particularly ignominious because the Falcons had a mere one safety in their 24–2 defeat, giving them the dubious distinction of being the first team in NFL history to score only two points in a playoff game.

Needless to say, it's not getting any cooler in Hotlanta for Matty Ice. While he has led the team to a winning record every year, Falcons faithful are ready for Ryan to truly ice the memory of Vick as a Falcon, and that means a deep playoff run.

CAREER HIGHLIGHTS

- ACC Player of the Year and winner of both the Manning Award and Johnny Unitas Golden Arm Award in 2007

- Offensive Rookie of the Year (2008)

- Named to the Pro Bowl in 2010

- Has the best career completion percentage (60.9) and quarterback rating (88.4) in Falcons history.

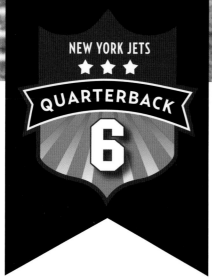

MARK SANCHEZ

While growing up in Orange County, California, Mark Sanchez's disciplinarian father Nick made Sanchez and his siblings recite multiplication tables and perform impromptu quizzes on the periodic table when they were in the batting cage or shooting free throws in the driveway.

"I wanted them to deal with difficult situations," says Nick, a former army sergeant. "My hope is that they would be stronger."

It, indeed, was good mental training for Sanchez. After a successful high-school football career, he chose to attend the University of Southern California (USC), where he backed up Heisman Trophy winner Matt Leinart. When Leinart graduated, Sanchez assumed he would lead the team — he was wrong. Coach Pete Carroll named John David Booty as his starter, but instead of transferring schools, Sanchez buckled down and eventually earned the starting spot, leading the Trojans to a 12–1 record in his junior year while throwing the second-most touchdowns in team history. Sanchez left school a year early, and the New York Jets selected him fifth overall in 2009, signing him to a five-year, $60 million contract, the richest in team history.

At first hailed as a savior by the New York media, it wasn't long before Sanchez was cut down to size. After a difficult loss in the sixth game of his rookie season to the Buffalo Bills in which Sanchez threw five interceptions, a newspaper printed the headline "Broadway Schmo." Sanchez took solace in a slice (or two) of cheesecake and slept in his car because he didn't want to go home, but he now has that

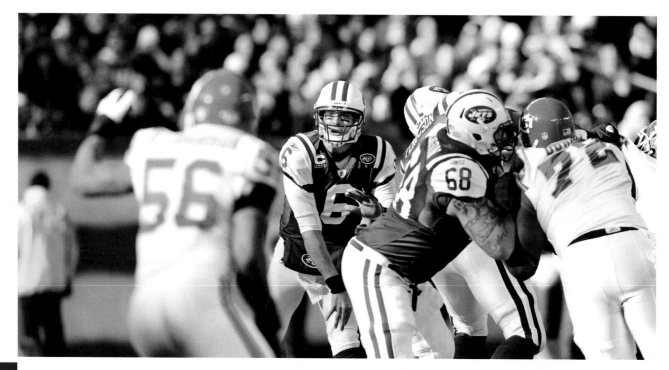

CAREER HIGHLIGHTS

- Tied in NFL history for the most postseason victories on the road (4)

- Record holder of the NFL's seventh-highest passer rating through a player's first six postseason starts (94.3)

- Set the Jets' rookie record for passing yards (2,444) and completions (196)

- Rose Bowl champion and Offensive MVP (1999)

- Parade and Super Prep All-American Player of the Year (2004)

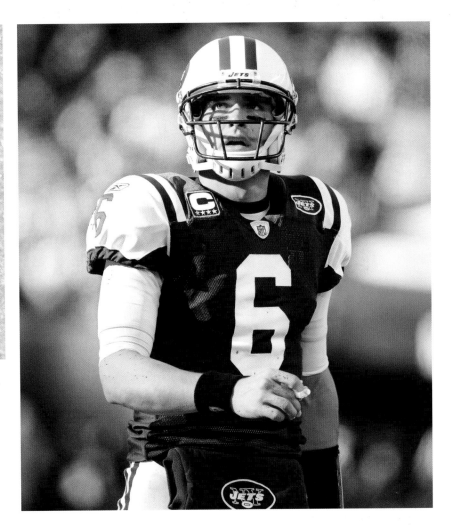

newspaper page blown up and posted by his bed as motivation.

Bouncing back, Sanchez, in his first two seasons, led the Jets to consecutive AFC Championship games, becoming one of only two quarterbacks to accomplish this feat.

Sanchez also threw 33 interceptions in his first two seasons, but Joe Namath — "Broadway Joe," the only man to lead the Jets to a Super Bowl — threw 42 in his first two seasons, and Sanchez has the legend's endorsement. "What I have seen of Mark these last two seasons, in my heart of hearts I know he's a champion-caliber quarterback."

IN THE HUDDLE

After reaching the AFC championship game in his first two NFL seasons, Sanchez is also first in Jets' history in postseason touchdown passes (9) and is only 11 yards behind Chad Pennington's team record of 1,166 postseason passing yards.

Namath famously guaranteed his Super Bowl victory in 1969, and in 2011, it was coach Rex Ryan who said the Jets would win the big one. They didn't come close, and with an 8–8 record, they failed to even make the playoffs.

Sanchez took more than his share of the blame as anonymous teammates criticized his work ethic and ability to lead the team. He did, however, have his defenders.

"Mark is the hardest-working quarterback I've ever worked with," says left guard Matt Slauson. "I mean, he is there all day long. He doesn't have an outside life … His whole life is about winning and improving the team."

Sanchez does get out, though, and where he goes is usually to a Broadway musical. He has become such a fixture on the scene that he has even presented a Tony Award. Explaining his affection for theatre in a GQ article, Sanchez said he feels a kinship with the regimented lives of the performers.

Reigning league MVP Aaron Rodgers called the article "embarrassing," but Rodgers operates in the league's smallest market as the quarterback of the Green Bay Packers while Sanchez

takes his licks in the biggest. And right now, for Sanchez, that means people like retired Jet and and ESPN analyst Damien Woody, want to see his leadership challenged.

"They definitely need to bring in a viable backup … because with competition, you are going to rise or you are just going to crumble," says Woody. "We'll see which Mark Sanchez shows up after that."

In 2012, the Jets traded for Tim Tebow, the backup for the Denver Broncos who took over the starting job and subsequently became the biggest story in the NFL as he led the Broncos into the playoffs. Sanchez has so far taken the high road. "He's been as advertised. [Tebow is] as good of a guy, if not better, than anybody said. I'm thrilled to work with him."

There's no telling if the tandem will be a success, but it certainly means the Jets will be taking center stage in the 2012 season.

—DETROIT LIONS
★ ★ ★

QUARTERBACK

9

MATT STAFFORD

CAREER HIGHLIGHTS

• NFL Comeback Player of the Year Award (2011)

• Third quarterback in NFL history with 5,000+ passing yards and 40+ touchdowns in a season

• Set the record for most passing yards (422) and touchdowns (5) by a rookie quarterback during a single game (versus Cleveland on November 22, 2009)

• Capital One Bowl MVP (2009)

When sports fans endure decades of futility they tend to blame their luck on supernatural forces. In baseball, for instance, the Boston Red Sox recently broke "the curse of the Bambino," and the Chicago Cubs are still hexed by a billy goat. The NFL has experienced this otherworldly phenomenon in Detroit, where Lions fans blame former quarterback Bobby Layne for their team's years of misfortune.

Layne was the last quarterback to win a title for the Lions (a pre–Super Bowl NFL championship in 1957), but in 1958, Lions management decided Layne's playboy lifestyle didn't fit the team image and he was traded. On his way out of town, he declared that the Lions wouldn't win for the next 50 years, and in the following years, the team won exactly one playoff game. Then, in 2008, on the 50th anniversary of the curse, the Lions secured the dubious distinction of becoming the first team to finish a season 0–16.

After this winless year, the Lions, ironically, turned to a graduate of Layne's former high school to break the curse. That man was quarterback Matt Stafford.

As a senior at Highland Park High School, Stafford threw for 4,018 yards and 38 touchdowns and led his team to the state championship. He was one of the most highly rated players in the country, and in Stafford's first two seasons with the University of Georgia, he led the Bulldogs to two Bowl victories, as well as to the top of the nation's rankings prior to his junior year. Losses that season to Alabama, Florida and Georgia Tech dropped Georgia from title contention, however, and the spotlight turned to fellow Southeastern Conference quarterback Tim Tebow of the University of Florida.

Stafford parted ways with Georgia after his junior season and in his wake left some critics underwhelmed by his college career. No matter — the Lions liked his arm and intelligence, and possibly his pedigree — and took him with the first pick of the 2009 draft. He won the starting job out of training camp and in the third game of the season helped the Lions win their first game since 2007 — a 19–14 decision over the Washington Redskins.

Stafford served notice to the NFL that he was to be taken for real later that year in a game against the Cleveland Browns.

During the game, he was wired for sound by NFL Films, and he didn't disappoint, throwing for a then-rookie-record 422 yards and tying the rookie single-game touchdown record with 5 touchdowns.

His final touchdown was dramatic. Stafford had suffered a shoulder injury on the last play of the game, but the Browns were called for pass interference, so he convinced his coaches to let him throw one more pass — it resulted in a last-second 38–37 victory. Afterward, NFL Films president Steve Sabol said Stafford "earned a lasting place in the cinematic folklore of the NFL," and praised him as having "the most dramatic player wiring ever."

In the opening game of his sophomore season, Stafford hurt the same shoulder and didn't return until Halloween, when he led the Lions to another win over the Redskins. A week later, he reinjured his shoulder and was out for the year after undergoing a procedure to shave his clavicle and repair his AC joint.

IN THE HUDDLE

Stafford is only the fourth quarterback in history to throw for 5,000 yards in a season (Dan Marino, Drew Brees and Tom Brady are the others). Stafford's 5,038 yards in 2011 ranks fifth all-time and he's the second-youngest player to accomplish the feat (after Marino).

Stafford came back strong in 2011 as the Lions rode his reconstructed joint with a league-high 66.4 percent of their offensive plays being passes. He also set all-time single-season team records in attempts (663), completions (421), yards (5,038), touchdowns (41), completion percentage (63.5) and passer rating (97.2), and was the winner of the NFL's Comeback Player of the Year Award.

The Lions finished second in the NFC North (with a 10–6 record), which meant they had made the playoffs. The faithful partied like it was 1999, which was, coincidentally, the last time the team had appeared in the postseason. But, like in 1999 (and 1997, 1995, 1994 and 1993), the Lions didn't last long as they ran into Drew Brees and the New Orleans Saints' buzz saw in the first round. Stafford threw for 380 yards and 3 touchdowns, but he was intercepted twice and the Lions lost 45–28.

With a core of young, dynamic playmakers on both sides of the ball, the Lions are poised to see more postseason action in the years to come, and fan excitement will, of course, be at a fever pitch with the 21st-century version of the swashbuckling Bobby Layne from Highland Park High at the helm.

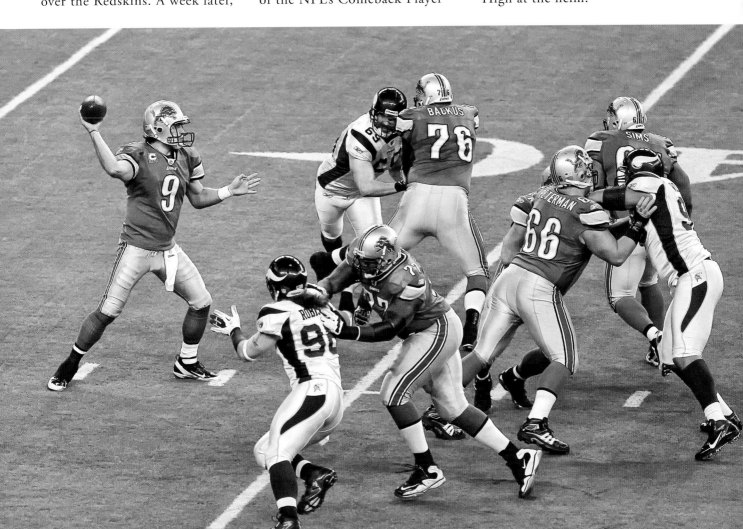

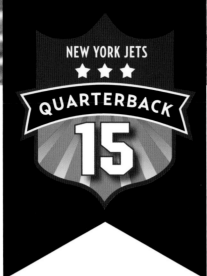

NEW YORK JETS ★ ★ ★

QUARTERBACK 15

TIM TEBOW

Believe. Tim Tebow does. America, however, was split down the middle in 2011.

Tebow was a late first-round, second-year backup quarterback when the 2011 season started, but before the year was out, he had seized the starting-quarterback role and the country had been swept up by "Tebowmania." Punctuated by what is known as "Tebowing" — the quarterback's method of on-field prayer, which he does with one knee on the ground and his fist to his forehead — athletes, celebrities and social-media society took up the act, both in homage and in ridicule.

It was this intersection of America's two precious Sunday traditions, football and religion, that made Tebow a pop culture phenomenon and the most hotly debated athlete in years.

The all-American Tebow was born in the Philippines (while his parents were doing Baptist missionary work), but he grew up in the U.S., where he quarterbacked Allen D. Nease High School, in Ponte Vedra Beach, Florida, to its first state championship.

As a starter, Tebow later led the University of Florida Gators to a 35–6 record and to two national championships (in 2007 and 2009). He also became only the second college player to consecutively win

the Maxwell Award (2007 and 2008), and he was a three-time Heisman Trophy finalist, winning it in 2007. Further, within the Southeast Conference, Tebow set career records for total offense (12,232 yards) and rushing touchdowns (57).

Tebow, however, didn't make believers out of the scouts. In fact, many of them suggested he become a running back or tight end because his awkward throwing motion produced as many wobbles as it did tight spirals.

IN THE HUDDLE
In 2007, Tebow became the first player in NCAA history to pass and rush for at least 20 touchdowns in a season. He was also the first sophomore to win the Heisman Trophy.

The Denver Broncos had faith, however, and they took him 25th overall in the 2010 draft. Tebow didn't get the reins handed to him until 2011, when the season was slipping away at 1–4 and with coach John Fox needing to change things up … or else. Tebow took the Broncos on a magical run with six straight wins, five fourth-quarter comebacks and three overtime victories.

Several of these wins were of the ugly variety and they included a 17–10 victory over the Kansas City

Chiefs in which Tebow had only two completions over the entire game. Further vindicating Tebow's detractors, the Broncos dropped their final three regular-season games (the last a 7–3 loss to the Chiefs that would have guaranteed a postseason berth).

Still, the 8–8 Broncos managed to sneak into the playoffs, where they faced the Pittsburgh Steelers and their top-ranked defense. With the teams tied 23–23 at the end of regulation, the ensuing overtime was the first under the NFL's new playoff rules: each team is awarded the ball unless the team receiving the opening kickoff scores a touchdown on its first drive.

The Broncos received the opening kickoff, and on the first play of the first drive, Tebow dropped back and hit Demaryius Thomas with a pass across the middle that he ran in for a touchdown. Eleven seconds into overtime, Tebow and the Broncos won a thriller as well as a boatload of converts.

But just when it looked like the Broncos were unstoppable, they ran into the New England Patriots, who trounced them 45–10 the following week. Then, in the 2012 off-season,

the Broncos' vice president John Elway persuaded Peyton Manning to come to Denver; suddenly, Tebow was expendable.

The Broncos dealt him to the New York Jets for a fourth– and sixth-round pick, which was a move that left many scratching their heads because the team had just given franchise quarterback Mark Sanchez a $40.5 million contract extension.

But, love him or loathe him, there's no changing the fact that Forbes named Tebow the second most influential athlete in America in 2012. Evidence of this was found during Super Bowl XLIV, when Tebow and his mother appeared in a commercial for a Christian pro-family advocacy group. Tebow's decision to participate in the ad only served to display one of the reasons he's embraced by some but is seen as a polarizing figure by others.

The Jets' locker room is just as divided, but for different reasons — some of the team's players publicly questioned Sanchez after the Jets missed the playoffs in 2011, so it only seems like a matter of time until quarterback controversy will begin to brew in the green half of New York.

Tebow will, of course, be at the eye of the storm, all the while earnestly believing in himself and having faith that he is on the right path.

CAREER HIGHLIGHTS

- Has two of the top three all-time single-game rushing performances by a Broncos quarterback

- Only the second rookie player in NFL history to run and pass for a touchdown in four games

- Two-time BCS National Champion (2007, 2009)

- Three-time All-American (2007–2009)

- Three-time Academic All-American (2007–2009)

- Winner of the Davey O'Brien Award for best college quarterback (2007)

- Two-time winner of the Maxwell Award for top college football player (2007, 2008)

- *Sports Illustrated* college football Player of the Decade

MICHAEL VICK

Michael Vick is one of modern sports' most polarizing athletes. On one hand, his career has been defined by his freakish physical ability, and on the other hand, he is most widely known because of his criminal conviction. Vick's recent comeback is a study in celebrity culture, as well as in public condemnation and forgiveness.

Vick grew up in a disadvantaged and dangerous part of Newport News, Virginia, where he avoided trouble by going to the local youth club after school and playing sports. His athletic prowess was obvious, and he escaped the housing project he grew up in by earning a football scholarship to Virginia Tech.

In Vick's freshman year, Virginia Tech had an 11–0 regular-season record and played in the national championship game, losing 46–29 to Florida State University, despite Vick throwing for 225 yards and rushing for 97 more. That season, Vick won the inaugural Archie Griffin Award as college player of the year and finished third in Heisman voting. However, because part of Vick wanted to provide his family with financial security, he left Virginia after his sophomore year and declared for the 2001 NFL draft.

The Atlanta Falcons selected Vick first overall, and in his rookie year he saw limited action. By his second season he was a Pro Bowl player and was firmly established as one of the best in the game. Everything went sour for Vick in 2007 when he was arrested and convicted on federal charges of financing and participating in a dog-fighting ring that allowed the killing of underperforming dogs. Vick served 18 months, had to pay back almost $20 million of his Falcons signing bonus and was released by his team after he got out of jail.

A free man and a free agent, Vick partnered with the

CAREER HIGHLIGHTS

- First player in Division I history to win league Player of the Year and Rookie of the Year in the same season (ACC, 1999)

- Four-time Pro Bowl selection (2002, 2004, 2005, 2010)

- NFL Comeback Player of the Year (2010)

- Holds the NFL quarterback records for 100-yard rushing games (11) as well as rushing yards in a single game (173), playoff game (119), season (1,039) and career (5,216)

Humane Society to educate children about animal cruelty. He also starred in BET's The Michael Vick Project, which is a documentary chronicling Vick's life after prison. Critics called it shameless self-promotion and a naked attempt to curry favor with the American public, but respected broadcaster and former Indianapolis Colts coach Tony Dungy believed Vick was truly changed.

Dungy took Vick under his wing, became his mentor and spiritual adviser and vouched for Vick when he was an NFL pariah. Eventually, the Philadelphia Eagles gave him a second chance, with coach Andy Reid citing his own family issues as one of the reasons for choosing Vick. Animal activists picketed the Eagles' training camp and came out in full force at home and on the road.

With controversy swirling and an absence from football for over two years, no one knew how Vick would play, and in 2009, he didn't get a chance to show anyone much of anything.

After serving a three-game suspension that was part of his violation of the NFL's personal conduct policy, Vick sat on the bench behind starter Donovan McNabb and patiently waited for a chance to prove he could still play.

IN THE HUDDLE
Vick was drafted by the Colorado Rockies in the 30th round of the 2000 Major League Baseball draft, despite not having played baseball since he was 14.

When Vick's moment came, he didn't waste it. On November 15, 2010, in a game against the Washington Redskins, Vick became the first player in NFL history to have more than 300 yards passing (333), 50 yards rushing (80), 4 touchdown passes and 2 rushing touchdowns in a single game.

It seemed like the better he played, the more forgiveness he was given, but he still remained a lightning rod for controversy. Before the 2011 season, ESPN

magazine published an article titled "What if Michael Vick Were White?" The piece included a picture of Vick with a white face and it basically asked the unanswerable question that if Michael Vick was another race, would the man, the talent and the controversy be the same?

Vick rose above the fray in 2011 and put up some record-breaking numbers. Twice more he passed for over 300 yards and ran for more than 50, doing so in back-to-back games against the San Francisco 49ers (416 and 75) and the Buffalo Bills (315 and 90). His season was unfortunately cut short by an injured hand, broken ribs and a concussion, which effectively meant the end of the Eagles' playoff hopes.

If Vick can lead the star-studded Eagles to their first Super Bowl victory in 2012, football fans will not only think of him as one of the sport's most physically gifted players, but also as one of the best quarterbacks in history. Earning the respect and forgiveness of the public, however, might not come quite as readily.

RECEIVERS

LARRY FITZGERALD — Arizona Cardinals

ANTONIO GATES — San Diego Chargers

TONY GONZALEZ — Atlanta Falcons

JIMMY GRAHAM — New Orleans Saints

ROB GRONKOWSKI — New England Patriots

GREG JENNINGS — Green Bay Packers

ANDRE JOHNSON — Houston Texans

CALVIN JOHNSON — Detroit Lions

STEVE SMITH — Carolina Panthers

WES WELKER — New England Patriots

KELLEN WINSLOW — Seattle Seahawks

JASON WITTEN — Dallas Cowboys

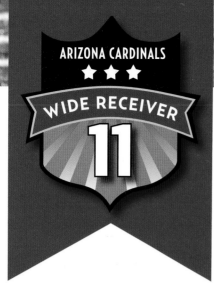

LARRY FITZGERALD

Hands aren't everything for a wide receiver, but they are definitely the main tool. At 6-foot-3 and 217 pounds, Minnesota native Larry Fitzgerald is regarded as one of the league's best-conditioned and most elegant players. He has tremendous leaping ability and body control, and he's known as "Spidey" for his sticky palms. The fact that he had

two of the hottest catching streaks in football history while playing with injured hands is even more remarkable.

The first streak came while Fitzgerald was a sophomore with the Panthers at the University of Pittsburgh. He had a torn ligament in his hand, but still managed 92 receptions for 1,672 yards and 22 touchdowns, won the Walter Camp

Award for being the best player in NCAA football, won the Fred Biletnikoff Award that honored the top wide receiver and found himself in the runner-up position for the Heisman Trophy.

Fitzgerald was the first player in Panthers history with back-to-back years totaling over 1,000 yards receiving, and when he left Pittsburgh after his second season,

Fitzgerald also had a school record of 34 touchdowns. He successfully petitioned the NFL to let him enter the draft despite only two years of college ball, and The Arizona Cardinals chose him with the third overall pick. It didn't take Fitzgerald long to establish his name within the NFL, and in the 2006 season, he became the youngest receiver — at 22 years and 123 days — in league history with 100 receptions.

Fitzgerald's father, Larry Sr., is a sports writer for the *Minnesota Spokesman-Recorder*, and that had its privileges for a young Larry Jr. He was a ball boy for the Minnesota Vikings, which gave him access to receiver Cris Carter, who became Fitzgerald's mentor.

IN THE HUDDLE
Voted one of the nicest players in the NFL by his peers in a 2011 *Sports Illustrated* poll, as well as the player most would want on their team to catch a Hail Mary pass. He also came out on top as the player voted best dressed.

Fitzgerald's life, however, hasn't been entirely gilded — in 2003, his mother died of a brain aneurysm while fighting breast cancer. Fitzgerald hasn't cut his hair since, and he braids it as a tribute to her. She remains an inspiration to him, and the example she set as a community activist explains how he stayed humble and gracious, even as he started shattering more records.

In 2005, Fitzgerald set a franchise mark with 103 catches, which broke Anquan Boldin's record in the same year the two wide receivers became the second set of teammates in NFL history to each have at least 100 catches and 1,400 receiving yards in a single season. In 2007, Fitzgerald had another 100 receptions for 1,409 yards and 10 touchdowns. He followed that performance by catching 1,431 yards in 2008, making him the fourth

receiver (Jerry Rice, Marvin Harrison and Randy Moss are the others) in NFL history to have at least 1,400 receiving yards in three or more seasons.

These accomplishments were merely a prelude to the 2008 postseason, which was when he launched himself to the level of superstar. After being held in check by the Pittsburgh Steelers for much of Super Bowl XLIII, Fitzgerald took over in the last 11 minutes, catching six passes for 115 yards and two touchdowns. Only one receiver had more yards in an entire game against Pittsburgh's top-ranked pass defense that year, and Fitzgerald's second TD, a 64-yard catch-and-run from quarterback Kurt Warner, gave the Cardinals a 23–20 lead with 2:37 left.

In that time, however, Steelers QB Ben Roethlisberger marched his team down the field and found Santonio Holmes in the corner of the end zone with 35 seconds left. Although Fitzgerald had one more catch, the Cardinals' final drive ended when Warner was sacked and fumbled the ball with five seconds left. Fitzgerald had set playoff marks for catches (30), yards (546), touchdowns (7) and TD catches in consecutive games (four), but he had fallen agonizingly short of his championship goal. It was later revealed, however, that Fitzgerald, with a broken bone in his hand, had somehow managed to break playoff records as well as win the Pro Bowl MVP award following the Super Bowl.

The Cardinals didn't make the playoffs in 2011, but surged in the second half of the season, and with a newly signed eight-year contract worth $120 million for Fitzgerald, the team is confident putting the future of the franchise in Fitzgerald's Hall of Fame–bound hands.

CAREER HIGHLIGHTS
- Named to five Pro Bowls, winning one Pro Bowl MVP award

- In 2009 became the first player in Cardinals history to have consecutive 10+ touchdowns in three consecutive seasons

- At 22 years, 123 days, became the youngest receiver in NFL history with 100 catches in a season

- At 26 years, 111 days, became the youngest player to reach 7,000 receiving yards

- Has nine TD receptions in six career postseason games, an NFL record for a player in his first six postseason games

- Holds the NFL single postseason record for receptions (30), receiving yards (546), and receiving TDs (7)

SAN DIEGO CHARGERS
★ ★ ★
TIGHT END
85

ANTONIO GATES

The prototype of the modern tight end is patterned after the Atlanta Falcons' Tony Gonzalez, who — with his height and leaping ability that made him a college basketball star — redefined the position in the NFL. Following closely behind him, and only a few years later, was the San Diego Chargers' Antonio Gates, who is another multidimensional tight end and former hoops standout.

Playing for Central High School in Detroit, Michigan, Gates was first-team All-State in both football and basketball, and he led the latter team to the state championship in his senior year. Basketball was so important to Gates that he later left Michigan State University when they insisted he focus on football. After bouncing around a few other schools, he ended up at Kent State University and busied himself with creating a legend on the hardcourt. In two seasons at Kent, he led the Golden Flashes to back-to-back conference championships and a berth in the Elite Eight of the 2002 NCAA tournament. Gates was the school's sixth all-time leading scorer and had his number (44) retired.

IN THE HUDDLE
There are currently seven modern-era tight ends enshrined in the Hall of Fame — Gates already has more career touchdowns than all of them.

These accolades weren't enough to convince NBA scouts, who believed the 6-foot-4 Gates didn't have the height to succeed professionally. In the face of this rejection, Gates scheduled his own workout in the summer of 2003 so NFL teams could see what he was capable of. Unbeknownst to most of the league personnel, however, Gates had sprained his ankle in a basketball game for prospects a week prior to his workout. He had a less-than-impressive showing, but Tim Brewster, the Chargers' tight ends coach at the time, knew about the sprained ankle and decided he had seen enough of Gates … on the basketball court. "If I had been truthful to the organization about what I saw that day," says Brewster, "we probably wouldn't

have signed Antonio." But they did, for a measly $7,000 signing bonus.

After not playing football since high school, Gates got his feet wet in 2003 with 24 catches for 389 yards. He proceeded to make a splash in the 2004 season with 81 receptions for 964 yards, setting the single-season touchdown record for tight ends (13) and by being named as a starter for the Pro Bowl as well as a first-team All-Pro.

Having Drew Brees at quarterback in San Diego certainly helped Gates' early development, but when Brees later left town, Gates hardly missed a step. Philip Rivers took over at quarterback in 2006 and Gates made the Pro Bowl and All-Pro teams again that season. The partnership between Gates and Rivers flourished. In 2011, they became the quarterback and tight end duo with the most touchdowns in NFL history, and Gates broke the franchise record for career receptions, finishing the season with 593. Both players have contracts that run through the 2015 season, not to mention

adjacent lockers, so, together, they might just put their records out of reach.

Gates is a nightmare to match up against, no matter who is playing quarterback, because he's too strong for cornerbacks and too quick for linebackers and safeties. Now that he's a veteran, he's also stopped relying solely on his natural talent and has become a more cerebral player, which was something he was forced to do in 2010 when a torn plantar fascia in his right foot spoiled his record-setting pace. He still, however, managed to have 10 touchdowns in 10 games to lead the team and make the Pro Bowl and All-Pro teams yet again.

"You can only do so much physically," says Gates. "You can only run so fast and jump so high. Mentally, there is an unlimited capacity on how you can grow. Mentally, the game seems slower."

Gonzalez's tight end reception record, which he's still adding to, might be unattainable for Gates, but if he can take the Chargers back to the playoffs and win a Super Bowl (which many

CAREER HIGHLIGHTS

- Named to the NFL All-Decade Team for the 2000s
- Named to the Chargers' 50th anniversary team
- Five-time All-Pro selection (2004–06, 2008, 2009)
- Eight-time Pro Bowl selection (2004–11)
- The Chargers' career leader in receptions

projected they would do after the 2011 season), he'll have a big one-up on the "Godfather" Gonzales.

The new crop of NFL tight ends, including Jimmy Graham (New Orleans Saints) and Rob Gronkowski (New England Patriots), are following in Gates' large footsteps. Both men had stellar 2011 seasons, but each has a lot of yardage to cover before they catch Gates — and there's the fact that they might not have his drive. As Gates once said, "I want to be known as the most exciting tight end to ever play this game."

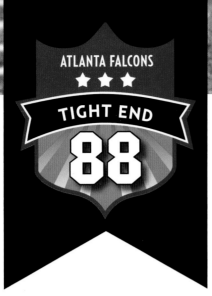

ATLANTA FALCONS
★ ★ ★

TIGHT END

88

TONY GONZALEZ

The term "legend" is thrown around a little too liberally in the world of sports, but in the case of the Atlanta Falcons' Tony Gonzalez, it can be used without hyperbole. Outside of quarterbacks Peyton Manning and Tom Brady, there are probably no active players who are more of a lock for the Hall of Fame than Gonzalez, and neither Manning nor Brady has defined his position the way Gonzalez has.

Gonzalez didn't set out to be a legendary tight end. "There was a time when playing football frightened me," he says. "I was kind of a geek and a coward. Girls ignored me." This admission is hard to believe coming from the man who was on ESPN's list of the world's sexiest athletes and who has appeared in numerous movies and TV shows, but it might take anyone a few years before they felt comfortable in a 6-foot-5 frame. He was also coming to grips with his diverse heritage, something he now takes tremendous pride in. His mother's family includes African-Americans, Caucasians and Native Americans, and his father's lineage is Jamaican, Portuguese and Scottish.

Not surprisingly, basketball was Gonzalez's first love, and while he was Orange County and Sunset League MVP in his senior year at Huntington Beach High School, he had, by this time, also become involved with football and was consequently named an All-American at tight end and linebacker. Gonzalez chose to go to the University of California, Berkeley to play both basketball and football, but he eventually chose to focus on the latter.

The Kansas City Chiefs traded up to draft Gonzalez 13th overall in 1997, and over 12 seasons with the Chiefs he went about breaking and setting most of the NFL's tight end records, including receptions in a season (102, in 2004), which was the same year he had a career-high 1,258 yards. He also changed the role of tight end from a blocking back and frustrated receiver to a first offensive option.

Two years later, in 2006, Gonzalez was diagnosed with Bell's Palsy (a form of facial paralysis caused by a malfunctioning nerve), but after acupuncture treatments and a radical diet change, he hasn't had a recurrence. Gonzalez remains a crusader for maintaining

CAREER HIGHLIGHTS

- Nine-time All-Pro selection (1999–2004, 2006–08)
- All-time leader in Pro Bowl receptions (49)
- Named to the NFL All-Decade Team for the 2000s
- First in career receptions among active players at any position and second all-time (behind Jerry Rice)
- Has only fumbled the ball once (in 2006) since 2000
- Named the Co-Orange County High School Athlete of the Year, along with Tiger Woods in 1994

a healthy diet and lifestyle, and is considered to be a model of fitness.

But the Chiefs didn't fully agree, and after the 2008 season they thought he was on the downside of his career. In exchange for Gonzalez, the team accepted a second-round draft choice from the Falcons. Gonzalez also felt he had run his course in Kansas City, and after a 2–14 season, he knew the team still had a big hill to climb toward lasting success.

In his three seasons with Atlanta, Gonzalez has remained consistently effective and often spectacular. In the 2011 season, at the age of 35, he was at or above most of his career averages and he made the Pro Bowl for the 11th time.

With Gonzalez's genes, passing Jerry Rice to become the all-time

leader in career receptions at any position isn't out of the question. Gonzalez needs about five more seasons in the game, and there's nothing to suggest he can't manage to achieve this. Fans in Atlanta will love if he sticks around until he's 40, but along the way they would also appreciate a few playoff victories.

IN THE HUDDLE
Gonzalez holds the NFL records for career receptions (1,149), receiving yards (13,338), touchdown catches (95), 100-yard receiving games (28), Pro Bowl appearances (12) and 1,000-yard seasons (4) by a tight end.

This is the one area Gonzalez falls short, as in three games with Kansas City and two with Atlanta

he's never won in the playoffs.

After the 2011 season, Gonzalez signed a one-year contract extension with Atlanta, so he has at least one more shot at postseason glory. Gonzalez, however, says making it to the Super Bowl isn't everything. "I would never look back and say, 'Woe is me,' and if I ever did, I'd kick myself … I have soaked this league up for everything it's worth. I've had fun. Made some great relationships. I don't regret anything."

A playoff win would be nice, though, and it would serve to burnish his legacy. "It would mean a lot to me," says Gonzalez. "I won't lie. But if you want to know how I'll feel, don't ask me after that game. Ask me after the Super Bowl." Because, of course, that's when true legends are born.

JIMMY GRAHAM

When Jimmy Graham was 11 years old, his mother decided she couldn't raise all of her children alone so she put him in the car, drove him to a group home and left him on the doorstep. Graham had two garbage bags of clothes to his name, and even though he wasn't a troublemaker, he was about to enter a facility for teens who had broken the law.

"Waking up in a place you don't know, with people you don't know, getting beat up every day — it sculpted me," says Graham. "I battled, but it's made my character." Graham had to fight for his food and often went without, so when he discovered a local church meeting that gave out free food, he jumped at the chance to become involved.

Teaching the bible classes was Becky Vinson, a young single mother trying to pay her way through school. She took Graham under her wing and eventually welcomed him into her home. "It wasn't like I was trying to harbor someone's kid," Vinson says. "He'd come eat and absolutely didn't want to go home. … Honest to God, in the winter, Jimmy would come to the house in shorts and knee socks. He only had three sets of clothes and one pair of pants.

He had holes in his shoes."

Vinson didn't have much money either, but she knew the value of hard work and the importance of schooling, so when Graham came home with failing grades, she told him in no uncertain terms that such a performance was not acceptable.

Graham improved and achieved As on his report card, which kept him on his high school basketball team. He excelled at the sport and was All-State before eventually accepting a scholarship to the University of Miami, where he was a two-time Academic All-ACC selection and earned a business degree with a double major in marketing and management.

On the hardcourt with the Hurricanes, Graham's athletic abilities were undeniable, and his 104 blocked shots are the eighth-highest in the school's history. As a result of his skill, he was offered a pro basketball contract in Spain.

IN THE HUDDLE
With 1,310 yards receiving, Graham joined Patriots tight end Rob Gronkowski (1,327 yards) in breaking Kellen Winslow's single-season tight-end yardage record (1,290) in 2011.

Miami's football coaches, however, had also taken note of Graham's rare blend of size, speed and toughness, and even though they tried to persuade him to join the team, it was university president Donna Shalala who convinced Graham to take graduate courses and try out a season of football. She even called in former Hurricanes quarterback and All-Pro Bernie Kosar to tutor Graham on the field.

"I could throw it 11 feet in the air and he'd still jump up 12 feet to get it," says Kosar. "I kept telling him, 'Jimmy, not only are

you going to be a great player, you're going to be a superstar.' He looked at me like I was an idiot or trying to be nice. But I just believed it from the first time I threw to him."

In Graham's first football season since ninth grade, he had a relatively modest 17 receptions with a 12.5-yard average and 5 touchdowns, but the New Orleans Saints saw the raw potential and drafted him in the third round, 95th overall, in 2010.

After scoring five touchdowns in his rookie year, Graham spent the off-season honing his craft with quarterback Drew Brees and other Saints teammates. The hard work paid off — in 2011, Graham was second in receptions in the NFC and he surpassed Kellen Winslow's single-season tight-end yardage record (1,290), finishing with 1,310 yards, which was only 17 yards fewer than the new record holder, Rob Gronkowski of the New England Patriots.

Graham's breakout regular season earned him a spot in the Pro Bowl and on the All-Pro team, and in two playoff

CAREER HIGHLIGHTS
- Pro Bowl (2011)
- All-Pro (2011)
- First tight end in Saints history with over 1,000 yards receiving
- Two-time Academic All-ACC (2006, 2007)

games he had 12 receptions for 158 yards and 3 touchdowns, including a 66-yarder against the San Francisco 49ers. The Saints lost that game when Vernon Davis, Graham's counterpart on the 49ers, caught a touchdown with only nine seconds left on the clock. It was a heartbreaking defeat, but both Graham and the city of New Orleans had experienced worse.

"That was one of the things I thought about right away about coming to New Orleans," says Graham. "I know there are a lot of kids in the city who have lived through a lot, and that seemed like sharing my own experience with them would be a kind of destiny."

ROB GRONKOWSKI

When the New England Patriots' Rob Gronkowski was fined $7,500 by the NFL for an overly emphatic spike of the ball after a touchdown, the Worcester Sharks of the American Hockey League (AHL) offered to pay the fine if he came and dropped a puck at one of their games.

It was a small price to pay to have the NFL's most successful young star show up at an AHL game, and just like he did for the entire 2011 season, Gronkowski did the unexpected at the hockey game — he broke the regulation puck into four pieces.

Such a feat of strength isn't actually surprising considering that power itself is the calling card of "Gronk" — the 6-foot-6, 265-pound tight end who is blessed with soft hands but who also has made a habit of bulldozing his way into the end zone, which he did a record number of times in 2011.

In the lead-up to the 2011 season, not many expected Gronkowski to rewrite the NFL record book, even though during his shortened two-year stint at the University of Arizona he had more receptions (75), receiving yards (1,197) and touchdowns (16) than any other tight end in Wildcats history. He had set the records in only 22 of his games, and even though he missed the entire 2009

season because of back surgery — a circumstance that lowered his stock as well as his draft position — he was still claimed by the Patriots in the second round, 42nd overall, in 2010.

An excellent rookie season in 2010 was a sign of things to come. Gronkowski's 10 touchdowns set team records for tight ends and first-year players at any position, and his touchdowns were the second-most

achieved by a rookie tight end in NFL history. Following 2010, the sophomore slump would have been an accepted phenomenon, but Gronkowski had no such problem.

"You probably missed out on what I did last year, but don't make the same mistake again," the ever-confident Gronkowski said to fantasy football players before the 2011 season. "Get ready to score some points."

Gronkowski lived up to his word. Going into 2011, the NFL single-season record for receiving yards by a tight end had stood for 30 years; that year, rookie Jimmy Graham of the New Orleans Saints beat it by 20 yards. Unfortunately for him, however, Gronkowski beat him by 17 yards more and now holds the new record at 1,327 yards.

Tight-end touchdowns are another story. Sure, the record wasn't 30 years old, but it didn't matter as Gronkowski didn't just break it, he shattered it. In the Patriots' 12th game of the season it looked like he had his 13th receiving touchdown to tie Antonio Gates' 2004 record, but one of his two on the day was ruled a lateral pass and scored as a rushing touchdown. The following week, Gronkowski made it official, and by the end of the season he held two different records — receiving touchdowns (17) and total touchdowns (18) by a tight end.

He didn't stop scoring in the postseason, either. Gronkowski tied an NFL postseason tight-end record with 3 touchdowns in the Patriots' 45–10 rout of the Denver Broncos in the divisional playoffs, and he had five catches for 87 yards in the AFC Championship game against the Baltimore Ravens. Unfortunately, on Gronkowski's last catch his ankle twisted grotesquely while he was being tackled. The Patriots, however, won 23–20, and the "high ankle sprain" became one of the top story lines leading up to a Super Bowl full of them.

IN THE HUDDLE

Gronkowski has two brothers in the NFL — Dan, who is with the Cleveland Browns, and Chris, who is with the Denver Broncos — and another brother, Gordie, who was drafted by Major League Baseball's Anaheim Angels.

Gronkowski couldn't practice in the two weeks before the Super Bowl, but after ditching his walking boot, being loaded with painkillers and having his foot heavily taped, he took to the field for Super Bowl XLVI. He was obviously hobbling, and after his historic season he was limited to only two catches for 26 yards.

Gronkowski gritted his teeth and played the entire game, almost putting the ultimate exclamation mark on his season. Down 21–17, Tom Brady's last-second Hail Mary pass was deflected in the end zone and fell just out of Gronkowski's reach. He had raced halfway down the field on an ankle as solid as his broken AHL puck, and, indeed, he went for surgery days after the game.

In the NFL, hard work and determination often transpire into good things — and with Gronkowski's threshold for pain, he should be a force for a long while yet.

GREEN BAY PACKERS ★★★
WIDE RECEIVER
85

GREG
JENNINGS

With Brett Favre and Aaron Rodgers as their back-to-back starters, the Green Bay Packers have boasted two of the best quarterbacks in NFL history. Wide receiver Greg Jennings has been the recipient of both their passes, and is either blessed to have caught them or is one of the reasons Favre and Rodgers have put up such impressive numbers.

In reality, it's probably a bit of both. After all, "Superman" (as Jennings was known in school) has a way of standing out all on his own. At Kalamazoo Central High

School in Michigan, Jennings was all-conference in football, basketball and track; he set a school record with 50 points in a basketball game and he was state champion in the long jump. Kalamazoo was also where he started dating his wife, Nicole, who he has known since fifth grade.

At Western Michigan University, Jennings went on to become just the 11th player in NCAA Division I history with three career 1,000-yard receiving seasons. In his senior year, he led the country with an average of 8.91 receptions per game and ranked second in the nation in yards per

game with 114.5.

The Packers chose Jennings in the second round, 52nd overall, in the 2006 draft, and despite being slowed by an ankle injury, he started 11 games and made the All-Rookie team. In the 2007 season, Jennings established a career high with 12 touchdowns (which he matched in 2010), and in 2008, he had his best year with 1,292 yards receiving, which was the first of three straight years he posted more than 1,000.

IN THE HUDDLE
Jennings caught Brett Favre's 400th career touchdown pass, as well as his 420th to tie Dan Marino's all-time record and then his 421st to break it. Jennings was also on the receiving end of Aaron Rodgers' first career touchdown pass.

Despite all of these accomplishments, it wasn't until the summer of 2009 that Jennings knew he had finally "arrived." The Arizona Cardinals' Larry Fitzgerald, arguably the best receiver in the NFL, invited Jennings to his native Minnesota to work out, and after spending time together, a mutual admiration was discovered and a fierce ping-pong rivalry was born; each continues to this day.

"Man, he's just so smooth in and out of his routes, the way he

catches the ball, how fluid he is, no wasted movements in his routes," says Fitzgerald of Jennings. "And then once he gets the ball in his hands, he's one of the premier guys in the league running after the catch. I mean, the guy, when he gets the football in his hands, he's just a tough person to get down on the ground, and he prides himself on that."

Only a sprained MCL kept Jennings from his fourth straight 1,000-yard season in 2011, and he finished with 949 yards and 9 touchdowns in 13 games played. His MCL did not keep him off the Pro Bowl roster, however, and he was the only selection out of Green Bay's very deep corps of receivers, all of whom had excellent seasons with Rodgers spreading the wealth with the 15–1 Packers.

Jennings missed the final three games of the 2011 regular season, but fought through his injury to play in the Packers' divisional-round playoff game against the New York

Giants. He had four receptions for 40 yards, but Green Bay lost at home to the eventual Super Bowl champions.

The loss prevented the Packers from defending their title, but Jennings has already secured his place in Packers lore — he had two touchdowns in the Packers' Super Bowl XLV championship in 2010 (the same year he was voted to the Pro Bowl for the first time); he has bridged the gap between Favre and Rodgers nicely, catching Favre's record-tying and record-breaking touchdown passes and Rodgers' first career touchdown throw (both in 2007); and since then, his career-receiving statistics place him among Green Bay's top 10 in all major receiving categories.

A devout Christian, Jennings has talked about retirement and how he might like to follow his father into the ministry or his mother into missionary work. He has also appeared on the TV shows Royal Pains and Criminal Minds,

CAREER HIGHLIGHTS

- Two-time Pro Bowl selection (2010, 2011)

- Super Bowl XLV champion

- Named to the All-Rookie team (2006)

- Finished his career at Western Michigan University first in career receptions (238), touchdown catches (39) and all-purpose yards (5,093)

- Mid-America Conference Offensive Player of the Year (2005)

and in 2010, he finished his degree in marketing with a minor in drug-abuse counseling. And, of course, there's always his burgeoning table-tennis career.

Whatever path Jennings chooses years from now, there's no doubt he will be first among equals because no matter what he does in life, he lives by his mantra, "Today is a great day to be great."

ANDRE JOHNSON

F amily is important to Andre Johnson — so much so that he trusted his uncle to act as his agent when he signed his first contract extension with the Houston Texans. His loyalty cost him money with a questionable deal; it proved to be one of the few false moves Johnson has made since he started playing in the NFL.

Johnson was raised by his single mom in a tough suburb of Miami, and after the eighth grade she decided to drive him half an hour each way to Miami Senior High School because she didn't like the company he was keeping at home. It was a wise decision, and as a senior Johnson caught 31 passes for 908 yards and 15 touchdowns, which earned him a scholarship with the local football powerhouse, the University of Miami.

Johnson wasn't the first receiving option when he arrived at Miami, but he was mentored by Reggie Wayne and Santana Moss — future NFL All-Pros — and by the end of Johnson's junior year he was fifth on the Hurricanes' all-time receptions list, third in touchdowns and only the second receiver in school history to break the 1,000-yard barrier in a season. His 10 touchdowns as a sophomore also helped Miami win the 2001 national title.

The Houston Texans loved Johnson's combination of size (6-foot-3, 226 pounds) and speed, and took him with the third overall pick in 2003. In his rookie year he was just 24 receiving yards short of 1,000, and in his second season he had 1,142 yards, prompting Hall of Famer Michael Irvin, another former Hurricane, to call the Texans' vice-president of communications, Tony Wyllie, and ask him to relay the following message to Johnson: "Tell him I want to marry him because I love his game so much."

In the years that followed, Johnson caught for over 1,000 yards four more times, leading the league in 2008 and 2009 with 1,575 and 1,569 yards, respectively. It was only the second time a player had led in back-to-back years since the NFL-AFL merger in 1970. In the 2010 season, Johnson maintained his torrid pace, averaging over 90 yards a game for the fourth straight season, but he ended up missing three games and the Pro Bowl with an ankle injury.

Johnson's 2011 season was both forgettable and memorable — he missed nine games battling a hamstring injury, but the Texans made the playoffs for the first time. It was sweet vindication for him after being on the outside looking in for his first eight seasons in the NFL. Having been with Houston for 9 of their 10 years of existence, Johnson was the longest-serving — and longest-suffering — Texan. Indeed, many had wondered if Houston was ever

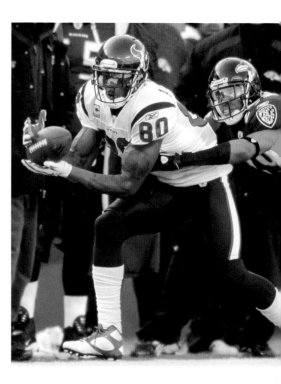

CAREER HIGHLIGHTS

- Five-time Pro Bowl selection (2004, 2006, 2008, 2009, 2010)
- Four-time All-Pro selection (2006, 2008, 2009, 2010)
- Three-time NFL Alumni Wide Receiver Of The Year (2006, 2008, 2009)
- Two-time NFL receiving-yards leader (2008, 2009)
- Three-time Houston Texans team MVP (2006, 2008, 2009)

going to make the playoffs, and if Johnson, the face of the franchise and one of the league's best players, was going to stick around until it happened.

"I always thought positive about it," says Johnson. "It's been some frustrating times and I've had people ask me, why didn't I leave? Why did I stay? I just wanted to be a part of something special. I wanted to be here when the Texans got in the first playoff game."

IN THE HUDDLE
Johnson ranks first in NFL history in receiving yards per game with 79.1.

In his debut playoff game, Johnson had 90 yards receiving and a touchdown in a 31–10 win over the Cincinnati Bengals. He bettered that with 111 yards against the shutdown defense of the Baltimore Ravens, but likely ended up spending the off-season lamenting Ed Reed's fourth-quarter interception of a pass that was intended for him — a

play that put the nail in the coffin of a 20–13 loss and that ended the Texans' title aspirations.

"There's a bigger goal than just getting to the playoffs," Johnson said at the time. "You can't be satisfied with it. The goal here is getting to the Super Bowl."

To come that close to the conference final with a third-string quarterback and without all-world defensive lineman Mario Williams is remarkable. It all bodes well for the future of the Texans, and Johnson will be a major part of the seasons to come, having signed a second, more equitable, contract extension with a new agent that will keep him with the team through 2016.

"Think about how long he's stuck it out here in Houston," says head coach Gary Kubiak, who arrived on the team a year after Johnson. "A lot of guys in this day and time move along, go somewhere else, lose their patience. Andre has never done that. He's been a rock around here."

DETROIT LIONS
★ ★ ★

WIDE RECEIVER
81

CALVIN JOHNSON

N FL nicknames are a great indicator of football success, and receiver Calvin Johnson earned them early and often. He has been called "Neo" (after *The Matrix* character who could slow down time and physically bend over backwards), "Unanimous" (as in an All-American selection), "Spiderman" (for his "sticky" palms and leaping ability), but the name that has stuck is "Megatron."

Contrary to the images this name produces, "He always had a kind nature about him," says Johnson's mother Arica who has a Ph.D. and works for the Atlanta school system. "He was the one to pick [opponents] off the ground. Sportsmanship was important to him." Armed with poise, impressive grades and a complete physical package, Johnson had his pick of schools but chose to stay in his home state and go to Georgia Tech. It was after only two games that he was known as the legend who scored two touchdowns in the final two minutes to beat Clemson University.

IN THE HUDDLE

Johnson has the most receptions (366), yards (5,872) and touchdowns (49) by a Lions receiver in their first five seasons with the club, and since 2008 has led the NFL with 45 receiving touchdowns, is second in receiving yards (5,116) and is tied for third with 49 receptions of 25+ yards.

"God touched him in so many different ways," said Buddy Geis, the receivers coach at Georgia Tech. "But Calvin works like He didn't give him anything." After setting most of Georgia Tech's receiving records, being named an All-American

(twice) and winning the ACC Player of the Year and Fred Biletnikoff awards, Johnson left after his junior season and was taken second overall by the Detroit Lions in 2007.

The Lions were an awful team when Johnson joined, and in his second year they became the first franchise to finish a season 0–16. He was their lone bright spot as he led the league in receiving touchdowns (12) and boasted 1,331 receiving yards that placed him fifth in the NFL.

It was with the Lions that former teammate Roy Williams dubbed Johnson "Megatron," urging the humble man in the locker room to change into a machine on the field. At 6-foot-5 and 236 pounds — and with a sprinter's speed and a basketball player's leap — it didn't take much effort, but lost among Johnson's circus catches is the fact that he is willing to sacrifice his body to block for his teammates.

Says the Lions' wide receivers coach Shawn Jefferson: "I'm talking about when that safety's barreling down, he sees you and you see him. I'm not talking about sneaking in behind somebody and getting them from the blindside. He

wants to be a complete receiver. And that means the non-talent issues like blocking. He doesn't know that he's a star in this league. He knows he's good. He knows what people say. But you watch this kid work … un-freakin'-believable."

Prior to the 2011 season, former All-Pro receiver Cris Carter thought differently when he said Johnson was only effective in video games. A month into the season, he changed his tune after Johnson tied Carter's record of four straight games with multiple touchdowns. "Right now, Calvin Johnson — there's a king in every crowd, and he's the king of the National Football League as far as wide receivers," recanted Carter.

At the end of the year, Johnson led the league in receiving yards (1,681), including the highest single-game total of the year (244) against the Green Bay Packers on the last day of

the season. He set career highs in yards (falling just five short of the Lions' franchise record), receptions (96) and touchdowns (16), and joined Randy Moss as the only receiver with over 1,600 yards and 16+ touchdowns in one season.

Johnson also shone when the season's spotlight was at its brightest; in the first playoff game of his career, he caught the ball 12 times for 211 yards and 2 touchdowns. Unfortunately, the New Orleans Saints outgunned the Lions 45–28, but it was the third time in four games Johnson went over 200 yards receiving, and in the process he set the record for receiving yards in the wild-card round of the playoffs and for the Lions' franchise in the postseason.

The Lions have a strong, young nucleus, including 5,000-yard passer Matt Stafford and defensive monster Ndamukong

CAREER HIGHLIGHTS

- Two-time All-Pro selection (2010, 2011)

- Three-time Pro Bowl selection (2009, 2010, 2011)

- Led the NFL in receiving yards in 2011 (1,681)

- Winner of the 2006 Fred Biletnikoff Award for the nation's top receiver

- ACC Player of the Year (2006)

- Two-time first-team All-American (2005, 2006)

Suh, and like the city of Detroit and its automotive industry, they're making a comeback. It also doesn't hurt, of course, to have the Cadillac of wide receivers driving the transformation.

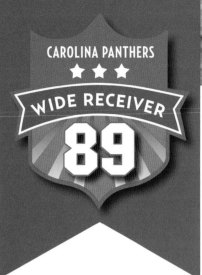

CAROLINA PANTHERS
★ ★ ★

WIDE RECEIVER
89

STEVE SMITH

In theory, a 32-year-old wide receiver who's 5-foot-9 and in his 11th NFL season should not be named to *Sports Illustrated's* mid-season All-Pro team and make the Pro Bowl at the end of the year, but Carolina's Steve Smith is driven by defying odds and proving critics wrong.

Blessed with dexterity, speed and a 40-inch vertical leap, Smith is tireless in his off-season workouts — it's the mental part of the game he has struggled with. It all started when Smith was an angry young man growing up in South Central L.A. — at one of his little league baseball games, his mother had to stop play and scold him for berating his teammates. Later, at Santa Monica College, coach Robert Taylor asked Smith why he was always so mad. When he said he didn't know, Taylor replied, "Well, until you find out, I'm going to sit your ass."

A one-game suspension didn't change Smith. He fought with teammates at the University of Utah (where he transferred after Santa Monica), and in 2002, during his second season in the NFL after being picked in the third round by the Panthers, he got into an argument with practice squad receiver Anthony Bright. Smith ended up putting Bright in the hospital with a broken nose, broken bones in his cheek and a damaged eye socket.

The gravity of this incident

got through to Smith, and he sought counselling with a sports psychologist. In a more outward sign of maturity, he also covered a tattoo he got in high school that read "Rough and Nasty, 100 Percent Fool."

"Steve's success is a result of his intensity," says former Carolina coach John Fox. "It's a fine line — that emotional, competitive mix. I don't want him to eliminate that part of him but to funnel it."

More focused in 2003, Smith led the Panthers with 88 receptions for 1,110 yards and 7 touchdowns and helped the team reach Super Bowl XXXVIII. In the divisional playoff against the St. Louis Rams, he scored the winning touchdown with a 69-yard catch-and-run in double overtime, and in the Super Bowl he caught 4 passes for 80 yards and a touchdown in a 32–29 loss to the New England Patriots.

IN THE HUDDLE

In 2005, Smith became the first player since Washington Redskins receiver Art Monk led the NFL in receptions in 1984, to lead the league while playing for a team that ran more often than it passed.

The following season (2004) also forced Smith to reflect on what he had and what he stood to lose. He broke his left fibula in the season opener and missed the rest of the year, giving him plenty of time to think. Upon his return in 2005, he won the receiving "Triple Crown," leading the league in receptions (103), receiving yards (1,563) and touchdowns (12). He also shared the NFL Comeback Player of the Year Award with the Patriots' Tedy Bruschi.

Smith now has a tattoo that reads "strong soul" in Chinese characters, and he's a dedicated husband and father who coaches his son's soccer team and dotes on each of his three children.

Though he's more circumspect, Smith hasn't completely mellowed. After a touchdown catch in a 2011 game, Smith took a late hit from Roman Harper of the New Orleans Saints, a scuffle broke out and Smith tried to lift Harper off the ground by his facemask.

Smith has learned, however, to keep his competitive fire between the lines of the football field. Instead of being brash and undisciplined, he used his passion to ignite a terrific 2011 season — one that no undersized, overage receiver has any business achieving, especially after it looked like he was almost finished in 2010.

That season, the Panthers had a 2–14 record and Smith, statistically, had his worst full season since his rookie year. At the season's end, however, he felt he had a unique opportunity for a fresh start in 2011, a year in which a new coaching staff and hotshot rookie quarterback Cam Newton were coming to town.

Smith was wise to stick around — he had the third-highest total receiving yards (1,394) and yards per game (87.1) of his career, and the second-highest yards per catch (17.6).

CAREER HIGHLIGHTS

- Carolina Panthers all-time leader in receiving yards

- Won the receiving "Triple Crown" in 2005, leading the league in receptions (103), yards (1,563) and touchdowns (12)

- Co-winner (with Tedy Bruschi) of the 2005 NFL Comeback Player of the Year Award

- Four-time Pro Bowl selection (2001, 2005, 2006, 2008)

- Three-time All-Pro (2001, 2005, 2008)

He also helped Newton become the first rookie quarterback to throw for more than 4,000 yards. Smith was motivated by those who said his career was over.

"His body and mind are tremendously competitive, as good as anybody I've ever been around," says former offensive coordinator Dan Henning. "If you're going to beat him, you're going to have to fight him to the death because he seems willing to go that far."

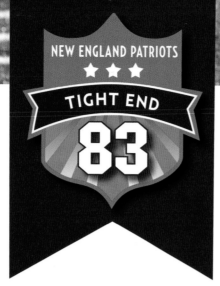

WES WELKER

Millions of kids dream of growing up to be an NFL star, but most of them will eventually look in the mirror and quietly realize they will never be as big or as strong or as fast as their idols. But to some of those kids, a supportive parent or coach will point out the New England Patriots' wide receiver Wes Welker for inspiration: He's the little engine that could and the patron saint of the pint-sized.

At just 5-foot-9 and 185 pounds, Welker appears to be built more like the soccer player he planned on becoming than the NFL superstar he grew to be. The stats, however, don't lie, and after four years at Heritage Hall High School, in Oklahoma City, Welker had 90 career touchdowns and had kicked a 57-yard field goal.

Welker's work in high school eventually got him named Oklahoma Player of the Year, but he didn't receive a single Division I scholarship offer. His father, Leland, suggested he try playing at a lower level, but Welker wasn't having it.

Finally, after a campaign by

Welker and Rod Warner (Welker's high school coach), he was offered a scholarship to Texas Tech University when another player backed out. Welker didn't disappoint, and he finished his collegiate career with school records of 259 receptions and 3,069 yards. He was also the NCAA career record-holder for punt return yards (1,761) and punt-return touchdowns (8).

Again, it wasn't enough, and Welker was passed over for the NFL scouting combine and went undrafted. The San Diego Chargers eventually signed him as a free agent in 2004, but he was waived three games into the season.

IN THE HUDDLE
Since joining the Patriots in 2007, Welker leads the NFL with a total of 554 receptions and 7.2 receptions per game, and he has the fourth highest single-season reception totals in Patriots history.

A week later Welker signed with the Miami Dolphins and he was finally given the opportunity to showcase his versatility. Before a 2004 game in New England, Dolphins kicker Olindo Mare suffered an injury, and Welker was pressed into duty. He converted a field goal and an extra point to become the first player in NFL history to record a punt return, a kickoff return, a field goal, an extra point and a kickoff in the same game.

The Patriots were only 3–3 against the inferior Dolphins with Welker in the lineup, so in 2007 Bill Belichick and the Patriots decided they'd rather have him on their side. They wouldn't regret the trade as Welker immediately meshed with All-Pro quarterback Tom Brady, who jokes that Welker "can hide in the grass." With Brady tossing the ball, Welker set a record for receptions (112) by a player in his first season with a team (rookie or veteran) in 2007. That number tied Welker for the league lead and as well as set the

Patriots' single-season reception record in the process.

In 2009, Welker led the NFL with 123 receptions (despite missing two games and part of another), which tied the second-highest single-season total in NFL history.

Unfortunately, though, after he made the tying reception in the final game of the season, Welker tore both his ACL and MCL while turning up field. He was as relentless in rehab as he is on the field and was, impressively, ready for the opening of the 2010 season.

Welker led the NFL in receptions for the third time in 2011 (he had 122 catches), but his season may well be remembered for the one he dropped. In Super Bowl XLVI, the Patriots were leading the New York Giants 17–14 with 4:06 left in the game. On second down and 11, Brady threw deep to Welker for what looked like a sure catch, but it bounced off his hands and fell harmlessly to the turf.

A reception could have iced the game, but the drive fizzled and the Giants came back to win the Super Bowl over the Patriots for the second time in four years. Welker was disconsolate after the game, and salt was rubbed in his wound when a New York–based company dumped 8,000 Butterfinger chocolate bars in Boston's downtown Copley Square with a sign that read "Thank you, Wes Welker."

The Patriots, however, decided that the 554 catches Welker has had since he joined the team beat his one drop — they designated him as their franchise player in 2012 and gave him a raise, which in turn provided 9.4 million reasons for pint-sized kids and teenagers to emulate Welker's drive, determination and willingness to prove naysayers wrong.

CAREER HIGHLIGHTS
- Four-time All-Pro (2007–2009, 2011)
- Four-time Pro Bowl selection (2008–2011)
- Holds the Patriots' single-season receptions record with 123, which is tied for the second-highest total in NFL history
- One of only two players with two seasons of more than 120 receptions; the only player with three over 110
- Tied a Super Bowl record with 11 receptions in Super Bowl XLII

KELLEN WINSLOW

The choice for a son to follow in his father's footsteps is never an easy one, especially when the son chooses to not only play the same sport, but also the same position, and the father is a Hall of Fame athlete. Comparisons are inevitable, and the fact that Kellen Winslow II has the same name as his father hasn't made things easier.

Kellen Jr. grew up in San Diego while his father was playing for the Chargers, but despite his genes, didn't play football until he was 14 because his parents were afraid he would burn out. He instead developed his athleticism playing basketball and soccer, all the while watching his dad redefine the tight end position and longing to be on the gridiron too.

The 2011 NFL season may have been one for the ages for tight ends, but it wasn't always this way. When Kellen Jr. was being recruited out of Scripps Ranch High School in San Diego, the position wasn't a featured part of many offenses and was often a dumping ground for misfits at other positions. Kellen Sr. insisted his son go to a school that put a premium on tight ends, and together they chose the powerhouse Hurricanes at the University of Miami in 2001.

Winslow was one of only four true freshmen on the Hurricanes' national championship team in 2001. He backed up Jeremy Shockey, future NFL All-Pro tight end and played alongside future NFL stars Frank Gore, Sean Taylor and Vince Wilfork.

IN THE HUDDLE
Winslow resisted the urge to name his son Kellen III, and instead called him Jalen Maximus.

After the Hurricanes won the national championship, Shockey left for the NFL and Winslow took over as the starter in his sophomore year. That season, he set school records for receptions (57), yards (726) and touchdowns (8) by a tight end.

In 2003, his third and final season in Miami, Winslow referred to himself as a "soldier" in a post game rant after a loss to the University of Tennessee. The backlash forced him to issue a statement apologizing to the men

and women of the armed forces and expressing embarrassment on behalf of himself, his family and his school. Despite the negative exposure, Winslow was voted a first-team All-American and won the John Mackey Award for being the best tight end in college football.

After courting controversy in Miami, Winslow found more in Cleveland. The Browns drafted him with the sixth overall pick in 2004, but he missed rookie camp while holding out for more money. He eventually signed a contract but ended up being sidelined almost his entire rookie season because of a broken leg. A year later, he crashed his motorcycle, tearing his right ACL and suffering a staph infection after his surgery. Driving a motorcycle was a direct violation of Winslow's contract with the Browns, and the team pondered voiding it or recouping the bonuses paid to Winslow. Ultimately, they chose not to do either and Winslow was welcomed back for the 2006 season after only playing two games in two years.

Never lacking in self-confidence, Winslow said during the preseason that he was operating at 90 percent, "But I think my 90 percent is still better than every tight end out there." He was vindicated during the 2006 season, scoring his first career touchdown in the Browns' opening game against the New Orleans Saints and leading the league with 89 catches by a tight

end, which tied him with Ozzie Newsome for the franchise record.

Winslow had microfracture surgery after the season to clean up his damaged knee, and in 2007 he had seven fewer receptions but finished with 1,106 yards, the highest of his career, and was named to his first Pro Bowl. In 2008, Winslow was hospitalized with another staph infection and missed six games, drawing the ire of the Browns by blaming the team for the rash of infections that had hit the organization (other players including Winslow had had infections in previous seasons.)

Winslow's outspokenness was a possible factor in the

Browns' decision to trade him before the 2009 season, a move that sent him to the Tampa Bay Buccaneers for two draft picks. Winslow made a splash in Tampa Bay, setting team tight end records in 2009 with 77 receptions and 884 yards receiving, and leading the team with 66 receptions in 2010.

Winslow had another strong year in 2011, finishing with 763 yards for the 4–12 Bucs. However, Tampa Bay decided to head in a different direction under a new head coach, and shipped Winslow to the Seattle Seahawks. With a competitive tight-end corps in Seattle, Winslow will have to be at his very best, a challenge he is looking forward to.

JASON WITTEN

Jason Witten is a reliable guy; in nine seasons as a tight end for the Dallas Cowboys he's only missed one game, and that was when his jaw was broken as a rookie and he required three plates to secure it. With his sure hands he's caught almost 700 passes for nearly 8,000 yards in his career, averaging 11.4 yards a catch while fumbling the ball only five times. Witten also goes about his business in as unassuming a manner as possible,

which is admirable considering he's on "America's Team." Witten just wants to contribute, and he's happy to do the dirty work, using his 6-foot-6, 265-pound frame to throw blocks for his teammates.

His demeanor may have something to do with his deep Christian faith and the perspective he gains through charity work. He volunteers with the SCOREkeepers program, which places positive male

mentors on staff at family abuse shelters across Texas, and he has lent his name and time to the Jason Witten Learning Centers that operate at Boys & Girls Clubs in East Dallas and in his hometown of Elizabethton, Tennessee. He and wife Michelle have also donated a hospital waiting room in Johnson City, Tennessee, and Witten runs the annual Jason Witten Football Camp, one of the country's largest free football camps.

CAREER HIGHLIGHTS

• Seven-time Pro Bowl selection (2004, 2005, 2006, 2007, 2008, 2009, 2010)

• Five-time All-Pro selection (2004, 2007, 2008, 2009, 2010)

• Three-time NFL Alumni Tight End of the Year (2007, 2008, 2010)

• Home Depot Neighborhood MVP (2008)

• Pro Football Weekly Humanitarian of the Year Award (2010)

• Dallas Cowboys Man of the Year (2007, 2008, 2010)

Playing for Elizabethton High School, Witten was a consensus All-American and USA Today Tennessee Player of the Year as a senior linebacker. He recorded 163 tackles, 9.0 sacks, 2 interceptions, 2 blocked kicks, 5 forced fumbles and 3 fumble recoveries, all of which was enough to earn him a scholarship to the University of Tennessee.

IN THE HUDDLE
Witten reached 600 receptions faster than any tight end in history, achieving this feat just 125 games. All-time tight-end reception leader Gonzalez took 134 games to reach the milestone.

True to form, Witten switched from defense to tight end when Tennessee was short and in need — and a legend was born. As a junior, he set the school's single-season tight-end records in receptions (39) and receiving yards (493), and one of his five touchdowns that season was the game-winning catch that sealed the Volunteers' victory against the University of Arkansas in the sixth overtime. Witten was also named to the All-SEC Academic team that season before declaring a year early for the 2003 draft.

The Cowboys took Witten in the third round, and by his second year he was a dominant player, leading the Cowboys and all NFC tight ends with 87 catches. He was also awarded the Cowboys' Man of the Year award in 2007, 2008 and 2010, as well as Howie Long's "Toughest Man in the NFL" designation following the 2007 season — an honor partly received because of Witten's legendary run against the

Philadelphia Eagles after getting his helmet knocked off by a tackler.

In 2010, Witten caught 94 passes for 1,002 yards (the third time in four seasons he had over 90 catches and 1,000 yards) and he was named a first-team All-Pro for the second time. The following year, after posting four consecutive seasons with more than 80 receptions and 1,000 receiving yards, Witten was one catch and 58 yards away from making it to five. He fell short, and so did the Cowboys, missing out on the playoffs by losing their final game to the New York Giants — the Cowboys' archrival. In November 2011, however, Witten passed Ozzie Newsome for third on the list of all-time receptions by a tight end. Witten now trails only Shannon Sharpe and Tony Gonzalez.

Prior to the 2011 season, Witten had the unenviable task of being the Cowboys' player representative during the

lockout. His teammates voted him in as a sign of respect and leadership, but he was put in an awkward position with owner Jerry Jones. After the lockout was resolved, Jones showed there were no hard feelings by signing Witten to a five-year, $37 million contract extension, making him a Cowboy for life. Witten will likely break Michael Irvin's franchise record for receptions in 2012, and if he keeps up his pace, he might also surpass Gonzalez to become the NFL's all-time leader for tight ends. It's a win-win for the team both on and off the field.

"This guy comes to work and wants to be the great football player every minute of every day," says Cowboys head coach Jason Garrett. "He wants to be a great blocker, a great receiver, a great teammate. He's a great example for me as a coach. He's a great example to everyone around the league about how to go about doing it."

RUNNING BACKS

★ ★ ★

MATT FORTE — Chicago Bears

ARIAN FOSTER — Houston Texans

FRANK GORE — San Francisco 49ers

FRED JACKSON — Buffalo Bills

CHRIS JOHNSON — Tennessee Titans

MAURICE JONES-DREW — Jacksonville Jaguars

MARSHAWN LYNCH — Seattle Seahawks

LESEAN MCCOY — Philadelphia Eagles

ADRIAN PETERSON — Minnesota Vikings

RAY RICE — Baltimore Ravens

★ ★ ★

CHICAGO BEARS
★ ★ ★

RUNNING BACK
22

MATT FORTE

CAREER HIGHLIGHTS

• Pro Bowl selection in 2011, despite playing only 12 games

• A total of 1,715 yards in his rookie season, a number that led all first-year running backs in yards and receptions and that broke Hall of Famer Gale Sayers' team rookie record for yardage in a season

• Tulane's all-time leader in rushing yards per game (99.2), rushing touchdowns (39), total touchdowns (44) and scoring by a non-kicker (266 points)

When Matt Forte was seven years old, he decided he wanted to be an NFL player. His father Gene sat him down and explained, "There are only 2,000 people in the United States who are going to play professional football every year."

Matt replied, "I'm going to be one of those 2,000."

Gene knew what he was talking about. In 1977, he was the football team's captain at Tulane University, and while he received offers to attend NFL training camps, he chose instead to take a job at Shell and settle down in Slidell, Louisiana, with his wife Gilda.

As the years went by, Matt grew into a high-energy kid who participated in soccer, baseball, basketball, gymnastics, karate and swimming. Forte's dad, however, tried to dissuade him from playing football, noting how his own knee surgery in college had been one of the reasons he cut his athletic career short and didn't attend the NFL camps.

Proving that the apple rarely falls far from the tree, Forte dominated the gridiron at Slidell High School, where he was district MVP and second-team All-State; he then chose to follow his dad's footsteps to Tulane.

One of only two schools to offer him a scholarship, Forte arrived low on Tulane's depth chart, but after proving his football intelligence and work ethic, he moved quickly up the ladder. Forte, though, had his own knee problems — he tore his posterior cruciate ligament and missed half his junior year before bouncing back in his senior season and rushing for 2,127 yards (the seventh-most in NCAA history), scoring 23 touchdowns and being named MVP of the Senior Bowl.

IN THE HUDDLE
Forte is the first running back in Bears history with at least 50 catches and over 1,400 yards from scrimmage in a player's first four seasons.

In 2008, the Chicago Bears picked Forte in the second round, 44th overall, and he turned out to be a steal. Forte set the franchise rookie records for rushing yards (1,238) and yards from scrimmage (1,715), breaking Gale Sayers' mark and leading the team with 63 receptions, which was a team record for running backs.

In his second season with the Bears, Forte suffered another knee injury, spraining his

medial collateral ligament, which robbed him of his speed and his first step. Forte, however, kept the injury a secret and didn't miss any playing time.

A healthy Forte bounced back in 2010, rushing for 1,069 yards and gaining a total of 1,616 all-purpose yards along with 9 touchdowns. In 2011, he was well on his way to a career season when he went down in the 12th game of the year with a Grade II MCL sprain.

At that point, Forte was leading the league with 1,487 total yards and was just three shy of 1,000 rushing yards. In his best game of the 12 he played, he ran for 205 yards against the Carolina Panthers, becoming the third Bears running back to break 200 yards (following Hall of Famers Sayers and Walter Payton into the history books). Forte was also on pace to break two single-season team records: Payton's rushing mark and

Sayers' all-purpose yards. Further, before Forte sprained his MCL, he was named the mid-season Offensive Player of the Year by *Sports Illustrated*.

Forte had accounted for 38 percent of the Bears' total yardage before he was injured, and this included a whopping 4.9 yards per carry. He was also a security blanket for backup quarterback Caleb Hanie, who was playing because starting quarterback Jay Cutler had broken his thumb. Without their two most dangerous offensive weapons, the Bears' season was doomed, and they lost five of their last six games, missing the playoffs.

At a salary of only $550,000 a year, Forte was one of the most underpaid players in the NFL in 2011, and heading into 2012 he and the Bears were at an impasse.

The team said they'd put the franchise tag on him, keeping him in Chicago for at least another year, but Forte wasn't

happy with that and skipped offseason workouts.

When the Bears signed running back Michael Bush it looked like Forte's time in Chicago was over, but the team envisioned both in the backfield and ended the contentious negotiations by signing him to a four year, $32 million contract on the eve of training camp.

The contract is a significant upgrade that will place Forte's salary where his play is — at an elite level, and well above what most of the 2,000 professional football players in America are making.

"The motivation is to provide for my family," said Forte before he signed the new contract. "You can't play this game forever. I like Chicago and you want an extension so you could play your whole career here."

Forte got his wish, and so did Bears fans everywhere.

ARIAN FOSTER

At 6-foot-1, 229 pounds and covered in tattoos, Houston Texans running back Arian Foster looks every bit the menacing NFL player, but proving a book can't be judged by its cover, Foster is the player who bows after scoring as a sign of respect to the game.

"Arian" is an abbreviated version of Aquarians, a name chosen by Foster's father that means "holder of knowledge." Foster is half Mexican American and half African American, and growing up he endured racial taunts and struggled with his identity and with his parents' divorce. He split his time between New Mexico and California, but still managed to excel at football, gaining 2,500 all-purpose yards and 30 touchdowns as a senior at Mission Bay High School in San Diego, feats that earned him a scholarship to the University of Tennessee.

At Tennessee, Foster was a philosophy major who studied Hindu teachings, poetry and yoga while rushing for 1,231 yards on a 10–4 team as a junior. In his senior season he had to share the carries, leading the team in rushing but with only 597 yards as the Volunteers sputtered to a 5–7 record in a year they were supposed to contend for the national title. These results got coach Phillip Fulmer fired and sent Foster's stock plummeting.

After going undrafted, the Texans signed Foster as a free agent in 2009, released him and then signed him to the practice squad. He was elevated to the active roster midway through the season and in six games he averaged a modest 42.8 yards per game, which was not a portent for 2010.

Foster got his shot as a starter in the first game of the 2010 season against the Indianapolis Colts, and he didn't waste the opportunity. He ran for a franchise-record 231 yards and 3 touchdowns on 33 carries, becoming the first player in NFL history to run for 200-plus yards and 3 touchdowns on opening weekend. It was the seventh-highest total in league history, and by the season's end, Foster led the NFL in rushing yards (1,616), yards from scrimmage (2,220), scoring by a non-kicker (108 points), touchdowns (18) and first downs (123), all of which were franchise records.

IN THE HUDDLE

Foster led the NFL in rushing in 2010 and recorded the most yards ever by an undrafted player with 1,616, surpassing Priest Holmes' previous record by one yard; Foster was also the third player in NFL history to amass 1,600 rushing yards and 600 receiving yards in a season.

In 2011, Foster missed three games with a hamstring injury, but he still rushed for 1,224 yards as the Texans leaned on him after losing both their first- and second-string quarterbacks (Matt Schaub and Matt Leinart), as well as All-Pros Andre Johnson and Mario Williams to injury. He also spent part of his bye week in New York City looking for a deeper understanding of the Occupy Wall Street movement.

With Foster carrying the load in 2011, the Texans reversed their 2010 record of 6–10 to win the AFC South. In their first playoff game in franchise history, Foster put Houston on his back, running for 153 yards and 2 touchdowns in a 31–10 victory over the Cincinnati Bengals. He added three receptions for 29 yards, accounting for 54

percent of Houston's offensive output.

The win over Cincinnati set up a showdown with the Baltimore Ravens and their vaunted defense, and once again Foster almost single-handedly won it for the Texans. He ran for 132 yards and a touchdown — the first player to gain over 100 yards against the Ravens all season and the first ever in the playoffs — but it wasn't enough as the Ravens prevailed 20–13.

"I just think he [Foster] has all of the tools," said the Ravens' Ray Lewis in 2011. "And then he's driven by a different burner inside. He was an undrafted guy with a lot of talent, so he is fueled by something different. Anytime you add that type of fuel with talent, you get Arian Foster."

Foster and Lewis are friends who formed a bond at the 2010 Pro Bowl, and they talked deep into the night after the ESPYs. Says

CAREER HIGHLIGHTS

- Two-time Pro Bowl selection (2010, 2011)
- Two-time All-Pro (2010, 2011)
- Won the NFL rushing title in 2010
- Houston Texans team MVP in 2010

Foster about Lewis: "Those kind of moments are just priceless to me because he's just a great human spirit, and anytime that you can be around people like that that inspire you, that's what life's about, is being inspired."

Not many players who have been on the receiving end of a Lewis hit or taunt would call him a great human spirit, and not many professional athletes would spend their time off with protesters, but then again, not many people are Arian Foster.

FRANK GORE

At Coral Gables High School, Frank Gore was a running back with raw talent who routinely rumbled over 100 yards — and sometimes 200 — in a competitive Florida league. Gore, however, was lazy, and even admits he was a "knucklehead" until his junior year, when coach Joe Montoya arrived.

Montoya challenged Gore to make the most of his talent and called him out in front of the team, which eventually culminated in an emotional private meeting between coach and player. Gore opened up about his struggle with a learning disorder and the challenges he faced being raised by his single mother in a small apartment that also housed several siblings and cousins.

"Frank cracked," according to Montoya. "He cracked to a point where he was going to quit. He was in tears. That's the way Frank is. He loves to play, but back then, he didn't know how to play."

After the meeting, Gore underwent a metamorphosis and became one of the hardest-working members of the team, challenging himself on the field and in the weight room against teammate Jonathan Vilma, who is now a New Orleans Saint.

Gore eventually followed Vilma to the University of Miami where, as a freshman on the national title team in 2001, Gore averaged an incredible 9.1 yards per carry on 62 carries. Running backs coach Don Soldinger, who had coached future NFL stars Edgerrin James, Clinton Portis and Willis McGahee, labeled Gore as "better than any of them."

"As far as his vision is concerned, [Gore] is probably the most natural of all of them," said Soldinger. "He

CAREER HIGHLIGHTS

- Three-time Pro Bowl selection (2006, 2009, 2011)

- All-Pro in 2006

- San Francisco 49ers' all-time leader in rushing yards (7,625) and 100-yard games (29)

- Set a new team record by rushing for over 100 yards in five consecutive games in 2011

- One of two players (along with Patrick Willis) to twice win the Bill Walsh Award (which is given to the 49ers' MVP, as voted on by the coaches)

runs low, he sees things other guys don't see. He goes to the daylight as good as anybody." Hurricanes head coach Larry Coker also once called Gore "potentially the best running back I've been around since Barry Sanders."

Gore, unfortunately, didn't get much of a chance to live up to expectations — he tore the ACL in his right knee before the 2002 season, and after a redshirt year to recover from surgery, he returned in 2003 only to tear the ACL in his left knee.

IN THE HUDDLE
Since Gore entered the league in 2005, he has more 100-yard rushing games (29) than any player in the NFL.

In a career that is based on speed and quick cuts, an ACL injury can easily put an end to everything. Gore, however, didn't let his knees get in the way of his success — he instead worked hard at rehabilitation and managed to end up seventh on the Hurricanes' all-time rushing list. Despite this achievement, his draft stock was still low and he fell to the third round in 2005, getting picked 65th overall by the San Francisco 49ers.

In his next five years in the NFL, Gore created a streak of healthy and productive seasons until he broke his hip in 2010. No stranger to rehab, he came back as strong as ever and justified the three-year extension the 49ers gave him 13 days before the 2011 season-opener. That season he earned Pro Bowl honors after running for the second-highest total of his career (1,211 yards), which included a team-record five straight games with over 100 yards and the surpassing of Joe Perry for the most rushing yards in franchise history (7,625). The team rushing record, however, took a backseat to what the 49ers accomplished that same day — a playoff spot for the

first time in Gore's NFL career.

After earning a first-round bye with a 13–3 record, the 49ers faced the Saints and won 36–32 with Gore running for 89 yards, including a 42-yard effort in the fourth quarter to set up a David Akers field goal. Gore also caught seven passes for 38 yards.

In the NFC final at home against the New York Giants, the 49ers lost in overtime in a 20–17 heartbreaker. Gore was beaten up after 16 carries (for 74 yards), 6 pass receptions (for 45 yards)

and countless blocks, and after six seasons of frustration it was difficult to be so close to the Super Bowl and not make it.

"It was a great year," Gore said immediately following the loss. "I just wish we could've gone to the big game, especially with all the hard work and all the tough times we've had."

If anyone knows the value of hard work and how to gain strength through adversity, it's Frank Gore, and if the 49ers follow his lead, they might go even further in 2012.

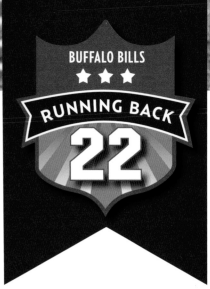

FRED JACKSON

Everybody loves an underdog, and they don't come much more lovable than Buffalo Bills running back Fred Jackson. Always considered too small or too slow, Jackson fought for every yard on his long journey to the NFL.

Jackson was the backup running back at Lamar High School, in Arlington, Texas, and his identical twin Patrick was behind him on the depth chart. As second– and third-stringers they weren't recruited by any colleges, but their middle school coach, Wayne Phillips, believed in them and found the Jackson twins a place to play.

Phillips had played in the 1950s for Bills coach Marv Levy at the Division III Coe College and had been a coach there himself in the 1970s. After the Jacksons' senior year of high school, Phillips drove them 12 hours north to visit the Coe campus in Cedar Rapids, Iowa. Despite a bit of culture shock, the brothers decided to attend so they could keep doing what they loved, and keep doing it together.

Fred rushed for 1,702 yards and 29 touchdowns and was named a Division III All-American as a senior, but NFL scouts didn't make it to many Coe games. After graduating, Fred (and Patrick, who was a defensive back) went to Sioux City, Iowa, to play indoor football for $200 a week on a thin layer of turf laid over the ice of a hockey rink. The Sioux City Bandits won a championship in their second season (2005), but Patrick decided to end his football career there, and instead chose to pursue a career as a youth counselor. He told Fred to keep chasing the NFL dream for both of them, and in 2006 Fred ran for 1,770 yards, which was a massive amount on a short field but was still not enough for the NFL to pick up the phone.

IN THE HUDDLE

Jackson's old neighborhood in Arlington, Texas, was demolished to make way for Cowboys Stadium, and in November 2011, Jackson played on the ground where his house once stood.

Fortunately, Jackson had the Levy connection and the Bills finally took a chance on him, sending him to play for the Rhein Fire of NFL Europe. After playing a season in Düsseldorf, Germany, Jackson was signed in 2006 to the Bills' practice squad.

On December 2, 2007, Jackson became the first Division III running back since 2000 to start an NFL game. That was his lone start in eight appearances that season. In 2008, he was a starter in three of the 16 games he played behind star running back Marshawn Lynch. A suspension handed to Lynch at the beginning of the 2009 season opened the door for Jackson. He seized the opportunity and rushed for 1,062 yards to become the first player in NFL history

to have more than 1,000 yards in both rushing and kickoff returns. His 2,516 combined net yards were the fourth highest single-season total ever.

Jackson was well on his way in the 2011 season — after 10 games, only the Chicago Bears' Matt Forte had more yards from scrimmage than Jackson's 1,376 (and, it should be noted, Forte's 15-yard lead came on 16 more touches). Unfortunately, however, 10 games were all Jackson played that year because he broke his leg in a game against the Miami Dolphins on November 20.

After Jackson's senior year at Coe, a scout for the Green Bay Packers told him he had talent, just not enough to make it to the NFL. Before the injury in 2011, the same scout tweeted that Jackson was carrying his fantasy football team, which earned Jackson the kind of vindication that fuels him.

"That 5'8", 145-pound high school backup is still out there with me," says Jackson. "I run angry. So I wouldn't change anything about my path because it made me the person and player I am today."

The fortunes of the Bills went down when Jackson did. They lost five of the season's last six games, ending up with a 6–10 record. The Bills showed promise early in the season, though, so Buffalo and its solid core of players shouldn't be counted out in 2012. As their overachieving running back has shown, with determination and the right opportunity, it's possible to defy the odds and become the top dog.

CAREER HIGHLIGHTS

- United Indoor Football League MVP and Offensive Player of the Year (2005)

- Set UIFL records with 1,770 yards rushing and 53 touchdowns (2005)

- Is one of only two players (along with Joseph Addai) to rush for a touchdown, catch a touchdown pass and throw for a touchdown in the same game

- First player in NFL history to rush for more than 1,000 yards and total more than 1,000 kickoff return yards in the same season (2009)

- Led the NFL with 2,516 combined net yards (rushing, receiving, kickoff, punting) in 2009, the fourth-most in NFL history

CHRIS JOHNSON

According to the NFL Players Association, the average career of a running back is 2.6 years, the shortest of any position on the field, so after his third season, Chris Johnson decided he wanted some security and held out for a long-term contract, one that would place him among the highest paid running backs in the league. After being drafted 24th out of East Carolina University and quickly becoming one of the elite runners in the NFL, Johnson had earned it.

"Quickly" is how Johnson does most things. In his senior year of high school, he finished second behind Walter Dix (an eventual bronze-medal winner at the Beijing Olympics) in the 100 meters at the Florida High School 4A State Championships, and at East Carolina, he wasted no time making his way into the record books, setting eight freshman marks, as well as being named to the Conference USA All-Freshmen team. Johnson put up a few more records before he graduated, but he saved the best for last. In the 2007 Hawaii Bowl against Boise State University, Johnson rushed for 223 yards on 28 carries, had 3 receptions for 32 yards and returned 6 kicks for 153 yards, all of which added up to an NCAA Bowl record of 408 all-purpose yards in a 41–38 East Carolina victory. It wasn't long afterward that at the NFL combine in his draft year, Johnson also set a record with a 4.24-second 40-yard dash.

Tennessee took notice of Johnson's speed and selected him in the first round. He finished the 2008 season with 1,228 rushing yards and 10 touchdowns in 15 games, his 81.9 yards per game led all the rookies, he was the runner-up in Rookie of the Year voting and he was named to the Pro Bowl.

IN THE HUDDLE
Johnson started record label "Flashy Lifestyle Entertainment" with his friend Kenny Turner, and spent the 2011 lockout recording a rap song called "Act on Deck."

The 2009 season cemented Johnson's status as an elite runner in the NFL — he joined a short list of legendary running backs when he ran for 2,006 yards, becoming just the sixth person in NFL history to run more than 2,000 yards in a season (he averaged an astounding 5.6 yards per carry and 125.4 yards per game). Also in 2009, Johnson's 2,509 all-purpose yards broke Marshall Faulk's single-season NFL record, he was voted the Offensive Player of the Year, and he earned a new nickname: "CJ2K."

After three seasons running for 4,598 yards (more than anyone else in the NFL), Johnson was set to be paid a relatively

paltry $1.065 million in 2011. To compare, Adrian Peterson of the Minnesota Vikings, who had 4,441 yards from 2008 to 2010, was in the middle of a five-year, $40.5 million contract.

"One day you're a real good back," said Johnson. "And the way I look at it, right now I'm better than all of them. Then all of sudden something happens to you, and you never did get paid. So why shouldn't I get paid now?" Johnson held out during the lockout-shortened training camp in 2011 and the Titans ended up giving him a four-year, $53.5 million contract with an opt-out clause.

Johnson started the 2011 season slowly, and after rushing for only 190 yards in his first five home games, the Titans faithful weren't shy about voicing their displeasure. Johnson, however, took the Bronx out of their cheers in

Week 12 when he matched his five-game total with a 190-yard effort at home against the Tampa Bay Buccaneers in a 23–17 win. The 190 yards were the most Tampa Bay had given up on the ground since Barry Sanders of the Detroit Lions gained 215 in 1997.

Johnson slipped to 1,047 rushing yards that season, and his carries also dropped from a career high of 358 in 2009 to 262 in 2011, which were almost 100 fewer opportunities to move the ball forward. Also, since many NFL teams are now shifting toward a largely aerial offense (the Titans threw for 476 times in 2009 and 584 in 2011), featured backs like Johnson are going to have to do more with less while also becoming more versatile offensively.

The aerial shift doesn't appear to be posing a problem for Johnson. In four seasons he's

CAREER HIGHLIGHTS

- Hawaii Bowl MVP (2007)
- Three-time Pro Bowl selection (2008, 2009, 2010)
- First-team All-Pro selection (2009)
- AP NFL Offensive Player of the Year (2009)
- NFL Alumni Running Back of the Year (2009)
- Rushed for 2,006 yards in 2009
- NFL-record 2,509 all-purpose yards in 2009.

averaged close to 50 receptions per year, and once the ball is in his hands his acceleration and elusiveness gain him a lot of ground. Johnson is in his prime at 26 years old, and if Tennessee hopes to get back to the playoffs, they're definitely going to need the speed of CJ2K.

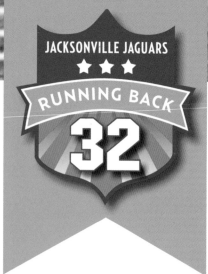

MAURICE JONES-DREW

The NFL is a league of behemoths, and when a player is only 5-foot-7, he's going to have to fight conventional wisdom. Running back Maurice Jones-Drew knows this better than anyone, and he wears No. 32 as a reminder of his early struggles. Because of his diminutive stature, Jones-Drew was passed over by all 32 NFL teams in the first round of the 2006 draft. The Jacksonville Jaguars eventually chose him with the 60th pick.

It was not as if Jones-Drew hadn't proven himself. As Maurice Drew, he went to De La Salle High School in Concord, California, and starred on a team that reeled off 151 straight victories, including a 29–15 win over Long Beach Polytechnic

High School that pitted the nation's top-two high school programs against each other for the first time. The game was on national television and it was a coming-out party for Drew, who scored all four of De La Salle's touchdowns, one of which had him somersaulting over a defender and into the end zone.

De La Salle did not lose a game with Drew on the team, and he ended his high school career ranked as the top all-purpose back in the U.S. He chose to move down the coast and go to UCLA, where he led the team in rushing during each of his three years there. He set the UCLA freshman record with an 83-yard run against Arizona State University, but this wasn't the only

school standard Drew claimed. He holds the career all-purpose yards record (4,688), the most single-game rushing yards (322) and touchdowns (5).

As a junior he set the NCAA mark for punt-return yardage with a 28.5 average, which was a remarkable achievement considering how Drew's season began. In UCLA's home opener against the Rice University Owls, he broke free for a 42-yard run in the third, but just as he was doing this, his maternal grandfather went into cardiac arrest in Section 3 of the Rose Bowl.

Maurice Jones was the man Drew grew up with and called "Pops"; he was the one person who went to every one of Drew's games.

CAREER HIGHLIGHTS

- Three-time Pro Bowler (2009, 2010, 2011)
- Three-time All-Pro (2009, 2010, 2011)
- NCAA single-season record — punt return average (28.5)
- Jacksonville Jaguars record — all-purpose yards in a single game (303)
- Jacksonville Jaguars record — single season all-purpose yards (2,250)

Jones was rushed to the hospital from the Rose Bowl, and when head coach Karl Dorrell told Drew what happened, he ran out the door but he was too late. From that day forward, Drew's jersey read "Jones-Drew" as a tribute to his Pops.

IN THE HUDDLE
Jones-Drew played the whole 2010 season with a torn meniscus in his left knee, but still managed to run for 1,324 yards and earn the right to be named Running Back of the Year by the NFL Alumni Association.

"When you're smaller than everyone else you gotta be able to do everything — play receiver, pass block, run block. You gotta take things personal," Jones once told his grandson. Jones-Drew took this advice to heart, especially when it came to the media bias toward the

University of Southern California program and its star running back, Reggie Bush, who won the Heisman that year (which he's since been stripped of for accepting cash, gifts and other impermissible benefits while playing for the Trojans), despite having fewer yards than Jones-Drew.

That slight was followed by the one on draft day, even though the Jaguars wisely chose Jones-Drew in the second round. After a relatively slow start to his rookie year, he announced his presence on the team in a game against the Indianapolis Colts in December 2006. Jones-Drew achieved team records of 166 rushing yards and 303 all-purpose yards. He also ended the season third in the NFL in kickoff return-average (27.7 yards) and touchdowns (16), while averaging 5.7 yards per carry, the highest in the league and most since

Barry Sanders was at the top with 6.1 yards per carry in 1997. Jones-Drew was snubbed one more time, though, and lost out to Vince Young in Rookie of the Year voting.

Now in his sixth season with the Jags, Jones-Drew has run for over 6,000 yards, has more than 2,000 yards in both receptions and returns, has scored over 70 touchdowns — including four in a game against the Tampa Bay Buccaneers in December 2011 to break the franchise record for career touchdowns — and has been named to three Pro Bowls and three All-Pro teams.

When NFL defensive giants wonder how the Jaguars' "Pocket Hercules" got over, around or through them for all that yardage and all those touchdowns, they just have to check the view because the inspiration is right there on his back as he scampers to the end zone: Jones-Drew, 32.

MARSHAWN LYNCH

CAREER HIGHLIGHTS

- Las Vegas Bowl MVP (2005)
- Holiday Bowl Co-MVP (2006)
- First-team All-American (2006)
- First-team All-Pac 10 (2006)
- Pac-10 Offensive Player of the Year (2006)
- Two-time Pro Bowl selection (2008, 2011)

On January 8, 2011, there was a minor earthquake in downtown Seattle. The ground below CenturyLink Field (then known as Qwest Field) seemed to be moving, yet there was no tectonic activity in the region — the source was the Seahawks' Marshawn Lynch rumbling downfield in his first career playoff game.

Lynch's 67-yard touchdown run in the fourth quarter, during which he broke eight tackles and knocked cornerback Tracy Porter to the ground with a stiff arm, was the winning score as the Seahawks shocked the defending Super Bowl champion New Orleans Saints 41–36. The crowd's reaction was so frenzied it registered on the Richter scale.

Having grown up in the Bay Area, Lynch is no stranger to earthquakes or to excited football fans. In his senior year at Oakland Technical High School, he ran for 1,722 yards and 23 touchdowns in only eight games, following that up with 375 yards and 10 touchdowns in two playoff games, earning him the San Francisco East Bay Player of the Year award in 2003.

Lynch stayed close to home to play at the University of California, Berkeley, where he became the starting running back in his sophomore year, racking up 1,246 yards and 10 touchdowns despite missing two games with a hand injury. He put an exclamation point on the season with 194 yards, three touchdowns and the MVP award in the Las Vegas Bowl in 2005.

Going into his junior year in 2006, Cal launched a campaign to get Lynch some Heisman Trophy recognition. Lynch fell short, but it's fair to say he went on to a more successful career than winner Troy Smith of Ohio State University, who's now playing in the United Football League. And so, instead of that year's Heisman, Lynch won the Pac-10 Offensive Player of the Year award and was named an All-American.

Forgoing his final year of college, Lynch was drafted by the Buffalo Bills with the 12th overall pick in 2007. The move to a colder climate didn't seem to faze him — Lynch became the first Bills' rookie since Greg Bell in 1984 to run for over 1,000 yards, and he broke the barrier on December 23 against the New York Giants.

Lynch finished with 1,115 yards in his rookie year and

followed that up with another 1,036 in 2008. Off-field issues halted the momentum, however. Lynch was arrested on drug and weapons charges three days after his appearance in the 2008 Pro Bowl. The felony weapons charge was reduced to three misdemeanors and no drug charges were filed, but Lynch couldn't escape the long arm of the NFL. Under the league's Personal Conduct Policy, commissioner Roger Goodell suspended Lynch for the first three games of the 2009 season.

During Lynch's absence, Fred Jackson stepped up and became Buffalo's starting running back, which eventually led to Lynch being traded to Seattle in 2010 and him taking them to the playoffs while keeping local seismologists busy.

In a play reminiscent of the "earthquake run," Lynch somehow escaped from a massive pileup for a 15-yard touchdown run against the Philadelphia Eagles on December 1, 2011. This was one of two runs he scored that day to effectively put the nail in the coffin of the Eagles' season. He was back in "beast mode," a term Lynch uses to describe his running style when he's locked in.

IN THE HUDDLE
On November 4, 2007, in a game against the Cincinnati Bengals, Lynch became the first non-quarterback on the Bills' roster to throw for a touchdown since 1981. During the game, Lynch had a 56-yard touchdown run and totaled 153 yards rushing.

After one of the touchdowns, a camera caught a trainer giving Lynch Skittles, a tradition dating back to when his mother rewarded him after scoring. Skittles was so happy about the exposure they offered Lynch a 24-month supply and a customized dispenser for his locker. Lynch ran for 148 yards against the Eagles during this game, which was the second-best performance of his career during the hottest streak of his professional life. He hadn't had consecutive 100-yard games until he did it four times in a five-game stretch in 2011, finishing the season with 1,204, his highest NFL total. Lynch also became the first Seattle back in five years to run for over 1,000 yards, breaking the second-longest team drought in the NFL behind the Detroit Lions.

Cynics might suggest Lynch got hot just in time to become a free agent, knowing he was in line for a lot more than Skittles. But, if he can help Seattle get back into the playoffs and continue to make the earth around Puget Sound shake, then he will be worth the investment for the team and for the fans who are buying tickets to enjoy the ride.

PHILADELPHIA EAGLES
★ ★ ★
RUNNING BACK
25

LESEAN McCOY

L eSean McCoy is quickly establishing himself as the football version of a closer, sealing victories and keeping the chains and the clock moving for the Philadelphia Eagles when the game is on the line. Since breaking into the league in 2009, McCoy has averaged 5.3 yards per carry in the fourth quarter, good for second among active NFL running backs, and 8 of his 28 rushing touchdowns — including his four longest — have happened in the final frame.

Eagles coach Andy Reid has a good explanation for McCoy's successes: "He's very young …

remember that. He's the one doing all the jumping around in the locker room afterward. I mean, he's riding a bike with 1:30 left in the game. He's got this phenomenal energy and loves to play. I joke around a little bit, but when he gets pulled out of a game he's not a real happy camper. He wants to be in there and he wants to play."

A native of Harrisburg, Pennsylvania, McCoy also had a youthful taste for candy when he entered the league. "I think since he grew up near Hershey, he enjoyed the fruits of the candy world," Reid says. "But he changed that and really dedicated himself to the profession. People who know football know how valuable he is to our team."

IN THE HUDDLE
In 2011 McCoy set franchise records and led the league with 17 rushing touchdowns and 20 total touchdowns; the last Eagle to lead the league in touchdowns was Steve Van Buren in 1947.

McCoy might have been hooked on sugar as a Panther at the University of Pittsburgh, but he still broke Dallas Cowboys legend Tony

CAREER HIGHLIGHTS

• Named an All-American and Big East Player of the Year in 2008

• Holds the Eagles team record for rushing yards and yards from scrimmage

• In 2010 was the only player to lead his team in both rushing and receptions, and he set a team record with a 5.2-yard rushing average

• Set an Eagles record by scoring a touchdown in nine straight games in 2011

• Has the best rushing average in team history (4.8)

• In 2011 led the NFL in first downs (102), 10+ yard rushes (48), rushing touchdowns (17) and total touchdowns (20)

• Named as starting running back for the NFC in the 2011 Pro Bowl

Dorsett's school record with 14 touchdowns as a freshman. He also ran for 148 yards in the 100th annual "Backyard Brawl," which resulted in a 13–9 Panthers victory over their rival West Virginia University Mountaineers, who, at the time, were ranked second in the country and were 28-point favorites.

In two seasons with Pittsburgh, McCoy rushed for more than 2,800 yards and broke the NCAA record for touchdowns (with 36) as a freshman and a sophomore, a record that had previously been held by the Arizona Cardinals' Larry Fitzgerald, a former Panther himself.

The Eagles took McCoy in the second round of the 2009 draft, and in his first year in the NFL he set an Eagles rookie record with 637 rushing yards on 4.1 yards per carry. After the season was finished, McCoy promised to pay more attention to his diet and conditioning.

In 2010, McCoy took a stranglehold on the starting running-back job, and without him the Eagles wouldn't have finished third in the NFL in points, second in total offense or first in plays of 20 yards or more. McCoy set an Eagles record with a 5.2-yard rushing average and was the only player to lead his team in both rushing and receiving. He wasn't named an All-Pro that year, but he did make the "All-Joe" team, an annual award given by USA Today to unrecognized overachievers.

If McCoy didn't quite get the credit he deserved in 2010, he forced people to sit up and take notice in 2011. He set an Eagles record by scoring a touchdown in nine straight games, and he led the NFL in first downs (102), 10+ yard rushes (48), rushing touchdowns (17) and total touchdowns (20). McCoy, however, didn't close out the season the way he hoped. He was fighting for the rushing title when he went down with an ankle injury in Week 16. McCoy missed the final game of the year and fell short of the rushing title, just as the Eagles fell short in their late-season surge for a playoff spot. McCoy did get in one more game, though, and that was as the starting running back for the NFC in the Pro Bowl. It was his first all-star game and it surely won't be his last.

The Eagles made a splash with their free-agent signings before the 2011 season, but it was their own second-round draft choice who was the season's breakout star in what turned out to be a disappointing year. McCoy has had an incredible start to his career, but in football it's not how you start, it's how you finish.

ADRIAN
PETERSON

"A.D." is a strange nickname for someone whose initials are A.P., so Minnesota Vikings fans call Adrian Peterson by the name they bestowed upon him during his record-breaking rookie season in 2007: "Purple Jesus." While coming from down south — Palestine, Texas to be exact — to fans of the Vikings he's been sent from above.

Peterson's father dubbed him A.D. because his hyperactivity as a child meant he could go "All Day."

He came by that fire honestly, when, as a seven-year-old he saw his eight-year-old brother Brian hit and killed by a drunk driver.

Brian was Adrian's best friend, and his death made him stronger. "When I think about how athletic he was ... I never could beat him in a race. He made all A's in school. Who knows what he might have been able to accomplish. [His death] motivates me to work even harder."

If that wasn't motivation enough, when Peterson was 13 his father was convicted of laundering money for a drug ring and sent to prison. Through it all Peterson just kept running, and college scouts noticed.

He chose Oklahoma and promptly set an NCAA freshman record, as a true freshman, with 1,925 yards rushing. The achievement earned him the second spot in Heisman voting, the highest a freshman has ever finished. Peterson played only seven games in his other two seasons as a Sooner, suffering a high ankle sprain as a sophomore and a broken collarbone as a junior, but still managed to come within 73 yards of Oklahoma's all-time rushing record.

After his third season he decided to declare for the NFL draft, and tragedy struck again. The night before the scouting combine his stepbrother Chris Parish was shot and killed. Peterson lay awake in his hotel room trying to comprehend what had happened and whether or not he should skip the combine altogether. In the end he listened to his agent, his mother, and the encouragement Parish had given him days before. He fought through the grief and shined for the scouts, showing them that

injuries and personal obstacles would not slow him down.

Minnesota selected Peterson seventh overall in the 2007 draft, and the Vikings faith in him was rewarded immediately. He rushed for 1,341 yards in his first season, including a 296 yard game against the Chargers, an NFL record. Almost by default, Peterson was named Offensive Rookie of the Year. He topped off his tremendous rookie campaign by winning the Pro Bowl MVP award, becoming only the second rookie to accomplish the feat.

Peterson hasn't slowed down a bit since, remaining one of the league's most explosive and durable backs, easily surpassing 1,000 yards in each of his five seasons. His career high came in 2008 when he ran for 1,780 yards and he has averaged 4.8 yards per carry for his career. In 2011 Peterson's Vikings were in transition after quarterback Brett Favre decided to call it quits, for good. Despite the Vikings' poor showing in 2011, Peterson still managed to post 970 yards in 12 games before suffering a season-ending ACL year. He was also rated the league's top running back and was third, behind quarterbacks Tom Brady and Peyton Manning, in overall player rankings done by the NFL Network.

IN THE HUDDLE
Peterson currently holds the third highest per-game rushing average in NFL history, behind Jim Brown and Barry Sanders.

Vikings coach Leslie Frazier, a former Chicago Bear, has invoked the name of legendary Bears running back Walter Payton when talking about Peterson, and Vikings personnel consultant Paul Wiggin has compared him to his own former teammate, Cleveland legend Jim Brown. It was a game in Cleveland in 2009, with Brown in attendance, that burnished Peterson's growing legend and produced what the Vikings running back calls his signature run: a 64 yard sideline dash with five broken tackles and two stiff-arms, part of a 180 yard game.

Peterson was bloody and dehydrated that day, and spent halftime vomiting, but Cleveland was one of the teams that chose not to take him in the draft and he had something to prove.

While some very good players were taken ahead of him, including the Lions' Calvin Johnson and the Browns' Joe Thomas, the six teams that passed on Peterson must still have a few restless nights, particularly before they face him. The team at the top of that list is the Oakland Raiders, whose choice to draft JaMarcus Russell first overall has made the club the NFL's version of the NBA's Portland Trailblazers, who famously picked Sam Bowie one spot ahead of Michael Jordan.

CAREER HIGHLIGHTS
- Most 200-yard rushing games for a rookie (2)
- Most yards rushing in a single game (296)
- 2007 Offensive Rookie of the Year
- Second rookie ever to win Pro Bowl MVP (after Marshall Faulk in 1994)
- Four-time Pro Bowler (2007 – 2010)
- Four-time All-Pro (2007 – 2010)

"The simple answer is [that] I think Adrian Peterson is the best football player in the NFL, so yeah, I don't think there's any doubt he's the No. 1 pick if you could re-do that draft," said Mike Mayock, a former NFL safety and respected NFL Network draft analyst. "You can talk about starting to build a team around a quarterback, and that's certainly valid. But this kid, he's the best running back I've seen in many, many years, and before he's all done, if he stays healthy, he could be the best of all time."

BALTIMORE RAVENS
★ ★ ★
RUNNING BACK
27

RAY RICE

There's a good reason Raymell "Ray" Maurice Rice can relate to the kids of New Rochelle, New York — not only did he grow up in New Rochelle, he continues to go back to the schools where his mother is a special needs teacher to spend time with the students and give them someone from the neighborhood to look up to. He is also aware of how difficult childhood can be and the importance of role models (Rice's father was killed when Rice was an infant, and a cousin, who stepped in to help raise Rice, later died in a car accident when Rice was in elementary school).

Rice persevered with his mother Janet by his side, but as a 5-foot-8 football player, he wasn't heavily recruited out of high school. He eventually chose Rutgers University, and despite the fact that Rice was a two-time All-State player, broke several Rutgers rushing records and carried the school into the national spotlight, when it was time to declare for the draft, he was not even considered as a first-round choice.

In 2006, Rice shattered Rutgers' single-season rushing record (with 1,794 yards), and he helped the team tie the school record of 11 wins. That season, Rutgers garnered its highest national ranking ever, finishing 12th after peaking at 6th. The team also won its first

CAREER HIGHLIGHTS

- Two-time Pro Bowl selection (2009, 2011)
- Two-time All-Pro selection (2009, 2011)
- Led the NFL in yards from scrimmage with 2,068 in 2011
- Set a Ravens franchise record with 15 touchdowns in 2011
- Since entering the league in 2008, Rice leads the NFL in receptions and receiving yards by a running back with 250 catches for 2,235 yards

bowl game in its 136-year history, beating Kansas State University 37–10 in the Texas Bowl.

A year later, in 2007, Rice was the first Rutgers player to run for over 1,000 yards in three consecutive seasons as he became the school's all-time leading rusher. He capped the season by running for a Rutgers single-game record of 280 yards and 4 touchdowns while leading the school to its second bowl championship (a 52–30 victory over Ball State University at the International Bowl).

After the International Bowl win, two-time All-American Rice decided to skip his senior season and declare for the draft. Thus, in 2008, the Baltimore Ravens drafted Rice in the second round, 55th overall. In his first season, he was part of a trio of backs that also included Le'Ron McClain and Willis McGahee, but by Rice's second season, he was the team's featured back.

Rice has also worked hard to become a receiving option, and in the 2009 season, his efforts paid off in a big way. He rushed for 1,339 yards and added 702 in the air, which made him one of only

two players with more than 2,000 total yards that season. Rice's performance earned him his first Pro Bowl and All-Pro appearances.

In 2011, Rice bettered both totals. On a team known for its suffocating defense, Rice was the offense, and not only did he have a career-high 1,364 yards rushing (good for second in the NFL behind Maurice Jones-Drew), he also led the team in receptions with 76 for 704 yards, which totaled a league-leading 2,068 yards from scrimmage. Further, Rice set a franchise record with 15 touchdowns in one season.

IN THE HUDDLE

In 2011, Rice became only the second player in NFL history to have at least 1,200 rushing yards and 700 receiving yards in multiple seasons. He joined Hall of Famer Marshall Faulk with this honor.

Also in 2011, the Ravens came within a missed field goal of making it to overtime in the AFC Championship game. This was a gut-wrenching loss, but one that Rice quickly put into perspective: "There are people in

the world hurting worse than the Baltimore Ravens. There are people with cancer; people suffering from poverty, disease. There are people battling real-life situations."

After coming so close to victory the Ravens didn't need to make significant changes in the off-season. By signing Rice to a new five-year, $40 million deal before he became a free agent, the Ravens have, according to *Sports Illustrated*, managed to hold on to one of only two "elite, every-down runners, with excellent pass-catching skills."

It will also give Rice a chance to become even more involved with his adopted city and further ingratiate himself with the people.

Following a visit with a Baltimore family who had won a trip to the Pro Bowl after being nominated for their community service, Rice was humbled: "[Their community service] means the world to me. We play a game, but there's people hurting a lot worse than I am after a loss. This is a time when I reflect on how blessed I am to play the game of football and to be able to get into the community and help out. It's very special."

DAVID AKERS — San Francisco 49ers

DEVIN HESTER — Chicago Bears

SEBASTIAN JANIKOWSKI — Oakland Raiders

SHANE LECHLER — Oakland Raiders

ANDY LEE — San Francisco 49ers

DARREN SPROLES — New Orleans Saints

SPECIAL TEAMS

SAN FRANCISCO 49ERS
★ ★ ★
KICKER
2

DAVID AKERS

San Francisco 49ers kicker David Akers is second in all-time postseason field goals (34), third in all-time postseason points and he's scored at least a point in all of the 20 playoff games he's participated in — an active streak that's the second-longest in postseason history. So, when the 49ers were set to receive a punt in overtime of the 2011 NFC Championship, they naturally liked their chances of continuing on to the Super Bowl. However, on the punt return, the 49ers' Kyle Williams fumbled the ball, gifting the New York Giants a short field goal and a trip to Indianapolis for Super Bowl XLVI. A dream season and a shot at glory had ended with one mistake.

Because of scenarios like this, there is intense pressure placed on kickers, so they need to be mentally resilient and tough, which are two qualities that Akers possesses and that have helped him become one of the all-time best. He has also dealt with his share of adversity, which has made him stronger in the face of stressful situations.

Akers was an All-State kicker (twice) while attending Tates Creek High School in Lexington, Kentucky, and he went on to become the second all-time leading scorer at the University of Louisville. He went undrafted in 1996, was signed and cut by the Carolina

Panthers in 1997 and the Atlanta Falcons in 1998. After being released by the Falcons he joined the Washington Redskins and actually made it to the 1998 active roster before he was released after one week and two missed kicks. Throughout these ups and downs, Akers was working as a substitute teacher and as a waiter at LongHorn Steakhouse.

IN THE HUDDLE
Akers is second in all-time postseason field goals made (34) and has scored at least a point in all 20 of the postseason games he's played in, giving him the second-longest streak in postseason history.

His first real kick at professional football was with the Berlin Thunder of NFL Europe, which was where the Philadelphia Eagles sent him after claiming his rights in 1998. Akers performed well enough to earn a tryout with the Eagles, but prior to training camp suffered a severe case of salmonella poisoning and lost 30 pounds as a result.

Akers bounced back and made the Eagles as the kickoff and long field-goal specialist. In October 1999, he kicked a 53-yard field goal against the Miami Dolphins, the first field goal of his career, and over the course of the next 12 years became the Eagles' all-time leader in regular-season and postseason games played

(188 and 19, respectively), points (1,323), field goals (294), 50-plus-yard field goals (15) and extra points (441). He also holds Philadelphia's franchise records for single-season points (144) and field goals (33), both of which he set in 2008.

The Eagles later let Akers become a free agent after he missed 41– and 34-yard field goals in a January 2011 playoff loss to the eventual Super Bowl champions, the Green Bay Packers. Akers, however, was dealing with an incredible burden that he had largely kept to himself — he had just learned that his six-year-old daughter Halley was diagnosed with an ovarian tumor. (Halley is better since surgery, but may face lifelong complications.)

The 49ers scooped up Akers for the start of the 2011 season, and in a classy move on his way out of Philadelphia, Akers bought a billboard that thanked his fans for their support and that he signed, "May God bless you all, David Akers."

San Francisco couldn't have been happier to sign Akers as a free agent.

In 2011, he set the NFL single-season record for field goals made (44) and attempted (52) and for most points with no touchdowns (166), helping the team go from 6–10 in 2010 to 13–3 in 2011. He also leapt to the defense of teammate Williams in the wake of the NFC Championship fumble.

"I'm irritated with the way people are treating him, absolutely. … Mistakes happen. We all make mistakes. But when you're out there truly battling to do the best you can, my hat goes off to him, to anybody that does that."

That kind of leadership comes as no surprise to 49ers head coach Jim Harbaugh: "I knew he was a great guy and a high-character guy, but I didn't anticipate what kind of a leader he was and what kind of impact he'd have on our team. I don't know if I've ever seen a kicker be as much of a leader as David has been. … He takes the time and works to get to know the other players on the team. I can't say enough about him. A class act all the way."

CAREER HIGHLIGHTS

- In 2011, set the NFL single-season record for most field goals made (44), most field goals attempted (52) and most points with no touchdowns (166)

- Named to the NFL's All-Decade Team after leading the NFL with 1,169 points in the 2000s

- Has scored 335 field goals and 1,478 points between 2000 and 2012, which is the most among NFL kickers within that time frame

- Six-time Pro Bowl selection (2001, 2002, 2004, 2009–2011)

- Six-time All-Pro (2001, 2002, 2004, 2009–2011)

- Won the Golden Toe Award (for best kicker or punter) in 2011

- Named to the Philadelphia Eagles' 75th Anniversary Team

CHICAGO BEARS
★ ★ ★

RECEIVER\RETURNER
23

DEVIN HESTER

Popular daydreams among sports lovers include scoring an overtime goal, hitting a walk-off home run and sinking a buzzer-beater that hits nothing but net. In the football world, the equivalent fantasy is taking the opening kickoff of the Super Bowl and running it back for a touchdown, and Devin Hester made the dream a reality when he did exactly that in Super Bowl XLI.

It's the kind of fantasy young Devin escaped to after his father died when he was 12. Legend has it that Lenoris Hester challenged the reigning Florida state 100-meter champion and had such a lead that he backpedaled the last five meters. Devin was the spitting image of his dad and inherited his speed, which he channeled on the football field to escape the pain of his loss.

Hester started his football career at Suncoast High School, in Riviera Beach, Florida, and in his senior year was the top recruit in the state. After receiving plenty of scholarship offers, Hester chose the University of Miami, and while there he became the first player in the modern history of the Hurricanes to play on offense, defense and special teams. He started games at cornerback, fullback, nickelback and running back, while also returning punts and kickoffs and getting spot duty as wide receiver.

"I've seen a lot of guys come through here," says Andreu Swasey, Miami's strength and conditioning coach. "But I don't think I've ever been around a guy this talented. You can't not find a position for him."

Unfortunately that versatility ended up working against Hester. NFL teams didn't know where he fit in and thought the fact that he played numerous positions in college was a sign that he didn't excel at any of them. When Chicago chose Hester 57th overall in the second round of the 2006 draft, many pundits thought it was a wasted pick. They were wrong.

In Hester's rookie year he had six return touchdowns, and no other player before him had ever reached more than four in a season. Each return touchdown was a highlight-reel play, but

CAREER HIGHLIGHTS

- Three-time Pro Bowl selection (2006, 2007, 2010)
- Four-time All-Pro (2006, 2007, 2010, 2011)
- Three-time NFL Alumni Special Teams Player of the Year (2006, 2007, 2010)
- ESPY Breakthrough Player of the Year (2007)
- NFL All-Decade Team for the 2000s

it was one in particular that announced to the NFL that a special talent had arrived. In a November game against the New York Giants, Hester fielded a 52-yard missed field goal, took two steps as if he was going to concede a touchback and then ran down the right sideline past the stunned Giants for an NFL-record-tying 108-yard touchdown.

While this was a definite highlight of Hester's season, it wasn't the peak — that moment came when he ran back the Indianapolis Colts' kickoff in Super Bowl XLI for a quick 7–0 lead. The Colts, however, wisely kicked away from Hester for the rest of the game and the Bears lost 29–17.

The following season, teams took the same tack and kept the ball away from Hester on 45 percent of their kicks. He persevered and still had six more return touchdowns (four on punts, two on kickoffs), and scored more points than any Bears receiver or running back.

However, with teams actively making efforts to keep the ball out of Hester's hands, the Bears needed to figure how he could become more involved. Hester wanted to play cornerback, a

position he thinks wins games and breeds respect from peers, but the Bears wanted their most dynamic player going forward, not backpedaling.

IN THE HUDDLE

Hester holds the NFL records for punt return touchdowns (12) and combined punt and kick return touchdowns (17). His 108-yard touchdown from a missed field goal does not count towards the record.

With his strong hands, quick feet and knack for making people miss, Hester became one of the Bears' best options at wide receiver, but when his return touchdowns dwindled in 2008 and 2009, fans complained that he was being stretched too thin and should be focusing on returns. Hester disproved the theory — in the 2010 and 2011 seasons he played in every game, averaged 26.4 yards a reception,

and scored five touchdowns to add to the six he scored on returns.

Further, in an October 2011 win over the Carolina Panthers, Eric Metcalf's punt-return record was broken when Hester achieved his 11th career punt return touchdown. Hester collected his 11 touchdowns in 182 chances; Metcalf's record of 10 had come on 351 punt returns. And, before the season was over, Hester added another punt return touchdown, plus a kick return touchdown, to increase his combined NFL record to 17 return TD's.

"Once he [Hester] gets the ball, anything can happen," says Detroit receiver Nate Burleson. "You've got to hope to contain him, not stop him."

If opponents of the Bears think they're going to stop Hester completely, they must be dreaming.

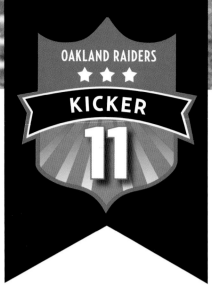

SEBASTIAN JANIKOWSKI

OAKLAND RAIDERS
★ ★ ★
KICKER
11

When Sebastian Janikowski was growing up, he wore the red and black of his favorite football team, AC Milan, who were not in NFL Europa but Serie A, Italy's top soccer division. Born in Wałbrzych, Poland, to a professional soccer-playing father, it seemed much more likely that Janikowski would end up playing European football, not the North American kind.

There have been a number of kickers in the NFL who grew up playing soccer, but what sets Janikowski apart is that he doesn't look like a striker — he looks more like a fullback. His

6-foot-2, 250-pound frame helps explain the power he gets from his left leg, and with his bald head and beard he cuts a menacing figure that isn't out of place among the diehard face-painters in the Oakland stands.

Janikowski, however, didn't kick an American football until he was a senior in high school. There wasn't much opportunity for that type of football in Poland, where he lived with his mother until he was 16. In 1994, Janikowski left his country for the U.S. where his father (who had left Poland years earlier to pursue his soccer career) announced he had married an American woman and could now bring his son overseas. Janikowski made the painful decision to leave his mother in order to join his father in Florida.

It was a difficult transition, as Janikowski had not seen his father in eight years and did not speak English. Janikowski felt like a fish out of water in Orlando, but his new soccer coach, Angelo Rossi, took him under his wing and convinced him to go to Seabreeze High School, in Daytona Beach, where Janikowski could play on a high-profile soccer team. He had to sit out for a season because of

transfer rules, so during that time Janikowski played in tournaments in Rossi's native Argentina, where he impressed with his size and skill and was offered a lucrative professional contract.

IN THE HUDDLE
Janikowski played on the Polish national under-17 soccer team as a 15-year-old and was offered numerous soccer scholarships after scoring 69 goals in 24 games as a high school senior in Florida.

Not eager to move to another country, Janikowski stayed in Daytona and in his senior year was convinced to kick for the football team. His distance became legendary, and fans lined the field to watch him warm up. Janikowski earned a scholarship to Florida State University, and in his three seasons as a Seminole he became the first two-time winner of the Lou Groza Award, which is the kicking equivalent of the Heisman.

Everything wasn't perfect at Florida State. Janikowski was known for his all-nighters drinking vodka and playing pool, and he was arrested for getting in bar fights and for attempting to bribe a police officer.

Undeterred, the Raiders drafted Janikowski with the 17th

pick in the 2000 draft, which was only the third time a kicker had been taken in the first round, and the first since 1979. In his early years in Oakland, Janikowski was given probation after an impaired driving charge and was arrested after a bar fight, but the charges were dismissed.

With age has come maturity, without a loss of power. In 2010, Janikowski set a team record with 142 points scored, after which the Raiders signed him to a four-year, $16 million contract, the richest a kicker has ever received. He was worth the money in 2011, when in the first game of the season against the Denver Broncos he tied the NFL record for longest field goal (63 yards) on *Monday Night Football*, and then set a team record with six field goals against the Chicago Bears in November. Janikowski has led Oakland in scoring in each of his 12 seasons

and has become the Raiders' all-time leader in points scored and field-goal accuracy.

Despite Jankowski's frequent and distant field goals in 2011, he couldn't kick Oakland into the playoffs, and his team lost to the San Diego Chargers on the last day of the season, missing a chance to get in as AFC West champions. The Raiders' intensely passionate fan base didn't blame Janikowski, however, and his prolific 2011 season earned him his first Pro Bowl appearance.

Larger than life, Janikowski is a hero from Oakland to Poland, and his on-field exploits just might convince some young football fans in his homeland to put down the round ball and take a kick at the oblong pigskin version. However, reaching the same level of talent as Janikowski might be tough. "It is something he was given at birth," says Rossi. "It's a gift."

CAREER HIGHLIGHTS

- Set an NFL record for the longest field goal in overtime (57 yards in 2008)

- Has the highest field-goal percentage in Raiders history (79.6%)

- Has led the Raiders in scoring in each of his 12 seasons, including a team-record 142 points in 2010

- Tied an NFL record with a 63-yard field goal against the Broncos in September 2011

- Set a career high with six field goals against the Bears in November 2011

- Named to his first Pro Bowl team in 2011

OAKLAND RAIDERS

PUNTER

9

SHANE LECHLER

Punter is not a glamorous position in the NFL. It's rare that punts are featured on the Sunday highlight reels or dissected by football's talking heads, and in Oakland, Raiders punter Shane Lechler takes a backseat to the bombastic leg and personality of place-kicker Sebastian Janikowski. True football fans, however, know that Lechler is likely the best punter in the business, and has been for over a decade.

Lechler could have focused on another sport (he starred in five of them in East Bernard, Texas), and he even showed promise as the quarterback for East Bernard High School, passing for over 5,000 yards in his high school career, but it was not meant to be.

When Lechler got to Texas A&M University he hoped to compete for the quarterback job, but coach R.C. Slocum had other ideas. "He was like, 'You know what? You're not going to want to hear this, but I want you just to be a punter,'" says Lechler. "That was hard to stomach because, quite frankly, I found it boring. There just wasn't enough going on. You go out to practice and you kick, and then you call it a day."

Lechler might have been

bored, but he excelled anyway. In his sophomore season he set the Aggies' record with a 47.0-yard punt average, and in his senior season he was named an All-American for the second time after nearly matching his sophomore record with a 46.5-yard average. His career average is an NCAA-record 44.7 yards, which includes six punts of 69 yards or longer.

In 2000, Lechler was drafted by the Raiders in the fifth round after they took Janikowski in the first round, which meant that in one day, Oakland had grabbed two of the best kickers in history, as well as two future franchise cornerstones.

During his 12 years in Oakland, Lechler achieved the six best seasons in Raiders punting-average history, his highest season coming in 2009 with 51.1 when he kicked for a team-record 4,909 yards. He topped 50 yards again in 2011 (with 50.8), which included the longest punt in Raiders history, an 80-yard effort against the Chicago Bears on November 27 that occurred during the same game that Janikowski also set a franchise mark with six field goals.

Janikowski didn't make his first Pro Bowl until 2011, but

Lechler has been in seven between 2001 and 2011. He has also been an All-Pro seven times and was named to the NFL's All-Decade Team for the 2000s. Throughout Lechler's years in Oakland, he has rewritten the Raiders' record book and owns the most important average a punter can: Lechler's career average of 47.6 yards is the best in league history and is more than two yards longer than charter member of the Hall of Fame Sammy Baugh's record. Baugh was voted in as a quarterback, though — a punter has yet to be enshrined. Lechler might eventually be the first, which is a speculation based not only on his numbers, but what they mean to his team.

As *Sports Illustrated*'s Peter King puts it, "Despite the punter's demonstrated strategic importance, he is often pegged as a pasty, emotionally challenged team pariah who stands by himself at the end of the bench with his arms crossed and his socks drooping to his ankles." At 6-foot-2 and 225 pounds, Lechler

doesn't exactly fit that archetype, and he's been given a little more respect than that by the Raiders, who signed him to a four-year, $16 million contract in 2009, recognizing that he might be their most valuable player.

IN THE HUDDLE

Lechler's family has athletic genes; his father played football and his mother played basketball, both at Baylor University; his brother punted for Texas A&M and he met his wife at Texas A&M while she was an All-American in volleyball.

While a well-placed punt might draw polite applause from the crowd, having to repeatedly march the entire length of the field to score can crush an opponent's spirit, and no one hits the "coffin corner," where the goal line meets the sideline and pins opponents deep in their own end, better than Lechler. In 2011, he downed 27 punts inside the 20.

With both Lechler and Janikowski making the Pro Bowl

CAREER HIGHLIGHTS

- Seven-time Pro Bowl selection (2001, 2004, 2007, 2008, 2009, 2010, 2011)

- Seven-time All-Pro (2000, 2003, 2004, 2008, 2009, 2010, 2011)

- Named to the NFL All-Decade Team for the 2000s

- Had at least one punt of 50 yards or more in 33 consecutive games from 2003 to 2005, the longest streak since the AFL/NFL merger in 1970

- Holds the NFL career average for punting with 47.6 yards

in 2011, Oakland has the best legs in the country. If the rest of the team could only play up to the level of these two men, there could be a Raiders renaissance — not just a kicking dynasty — setting the franchise up for glory.

SAN FRANCISCO 49ERS
★ ★ ★
PUNTER
4

ANDY LEE

The Oakland Raiders' Shane Lechler has set the gold standard for punters for over a decade now, but just across the bay he has some serious competition in the San Francisco 49ers' Andy Lee.

In 2011, Lee and Lechler had the exact same number of punts, but Lee nipped Lechler at the post, beating his average by a tenth of a yard for the highest in the NFL at 50.9. He also beat Lechler, 28 to 27, on total punts landed inside the opponent's 20 yard line. As a result, opponents of the 49ers had to start, on average, deeper in their own half than against any other team in the league; a huge advantage for a team that went from 6–10 in 2010 to 13–3 in 2011.

Growing up in Westminster, South Carolina, Lee didn't picture earning his living with his right leg; instead, he hoped it would be with his right arm. Lee admits he was more into baseball, and as a high school pitcher was clocked with a 91 mile-per-hour fastball, going 5–0 as a junior and earning All-State honors with an 8–2 record as a senior. He was also a pretty fair hitter, with a .460 batting average in his final season.

Lee did, however, punt for the football team, and he also played tight end and wide receiver. His 42.8-yard average in his senior year earned him a scholarship to the University of Pittsburgh, and in four years as

the first-string punter, Lee set school records with 244 punts and 10,353 yards, and was the first player in conference history to twice win the Big East Special Teams Player of the Year Award.

Lee's first live NFL game — watching or participating — was experienced during his debut in a San Francisco uniform, after the team chose him in the sixth round of the 2004 draft. That season he kicked an 81-yarder against Tampa Bay and became the first 49er since 1957 to have the longest punt in the league as a rookie.

By 2007, Lee was firmly established in the NFL, having set numerous single-season team records, as well as an NFL record with 42 punts downed inside the opponent's 20; he had also earned his first Pro Bowl and All-Pro honors.

Lee's numbers have only continued to rise, and in 2011, he broke the long-held 1976 NFL record for net average. He did it by punting for a 59.6-yard average in Week 1 (third-best in league history) and concluding the regular season with a 64-yarder in St. Louis, which was downed at the 1-yard line to

finish Lee's year leading in both gross and net punting yardage. He was also named to his third Pro Bowl and third All-Pro team, and now holds the franchise record in eight of ten punting categories.

IN THE HUDDLE

Lee was given the key to his hometown of Westminster, South Carolina, and July 12 is now "Andy Lee Day."

While Lee still misses baseball, he says he made the right choice and, in fact, his growth as a punter has been attributed to his background as a pitcher and all-around athlete.

His training has also been beneficial in his side job as the holder for teammate David Akers' field goals and extra points.

"He had a different mind-set and demeanor than many college punters and kickers, because he's a really good athlete," says Bryan Deal, who was the special teams coach when Lee was in Pittsburgh. "He liked the pressure. Bottom of the ninth, he wanted the ball hit to him — and he wanted the pressure of a big kick."

With the punter and kicker of

CAREER HIGHLIGHTS

- The only player ever to twice win the Big East Special Teams Player of the Year Award

- Ranks first in 49ers history in punts (723), yards (33,069), gross average (45.7), net average (39.0) and punts inside the 20 (209)

- Three-time All-Pro (2007, 2009, 2011)

- Three-time Pro Bowl selection (2007, 2009, 2011)

both the Raiders and 49ers making the Pro Bowl and All-Pro team in 2011, the Bay Area is now the epicenter of the kicking world. Unlike the Raiders, however, the 49ers won their division and made the playoffs.

Lee has a middle-of-the-pack contract that ends after the 2012 season; if the 49ers hope to retain him, and keep opponents deep in their own end, they're going to need to pay him like his Bay Area brethren. Lee has, after all, shown that he's their equal — he might even have a leg up on them.

DARREN SPROLES

NEW ORLEANS SAINTS
★ ★ ★
RETURN SPECIALIST
43

Darren Sproles came into the world big. He was 10 pounds at birth and subsequently nicknamed "Tank," but the joke now is that he's actually the shortest player in the NFL at 5-foot-6 and weighing in at 190 pounds. His play on the field, however, lends credence to the adage that it's not possible to measure the size of a heart.

Sproles gave it his all from an early age (his peewee football league passed a rule against running sweeps because Sproles scored a touchdown every single time he ran one), and when in high school, Sproles rushed for 5,230 yards (averaging 8.4 yards per carry) and scored 79 touchdowns. In 2003 he led the country in rushing during his junior season at Kansas State University and helped the Wildcats upset the heavily favored and top-ranked University of Oklahoma in the Big 12 Championship.

After finishing fifth in Heisman voting that year, Sproles could have declared early for the NFL draft, but he instead chose to keep a promise to his mother, Annette, that he would finish his degree. Unfortunately, she lost her five-year battle with cancer at the beginning of Sproles' senior year, and even though he played that season with a heavy heart, he finished his collegiate career with 23 school records, in 11th place on the all-time NCAA rushing yards list and sixth in all-purpose yards.

Sproles also earned his degree in Speech Pathology, a subject close to his heart because he'd always struggled with a stutter. It was a problem that affected his confidence and made him uncomfortable when it came to dealing with the media that followed in the wake of his gridiron success. It was also one that endeared him to coaches and

teammates as much as his oversized achievements on the field did.

Sproles was drafted by the San Diego Chargers in the fourth round of the 2005 draft, and even though the team boasted a player like LaDainian Tomlinson, who was the best running back in the game at the time, Sproles didn't complain. In six years with the Chargers, he carried the ball 249 times for 1,154 yards (a 4.6-yard average), had 146 receptions for 1,400 yards and while on special teams returned 25 kickoffs for 6,469 yards (a 25.1-yard average) and returned 114 punts for 935 yards.

IN THE HUDDLE
Since 2007, Sproles has collected 10,956 all-purpose yards, which is an NFL record.

With stats like that, it's no wonder Sproles still goes by the nickname "Tank." He's not afraid to block men almost twice his weight and he doesn't hesitate to chew up large chunks of the field, a fact that was proven in a playoff game against the Indianapolis Colts in 2008 when Sproles accounted for 328 all-purpose yards (105 rushing, 45 receiving, 106 kick returning and 72 punt returning) and made the play on the winning touchdown in a 23–17 overtime win.

Moving forward into 2009, the Chargers placed the franchise tag on Sproles, but in 2011, the New Orleans Saints signed him as a free agent, replacing the departed Reggie Bush and reuniting Sproles with former Chargers quarterback Drew Brees.

The former chemistry between Sproles and Brees was easy to recreate, and Sproles was an instant Saints success. In his first game with the team, he returned a kick for a touchdown against the Green Bay Packers, and by his fourth game he already had more than 1,000 all-purpose yards. Further, in the second-last game of the year, Sproles caught the pass that Brees threw to break Dan Marino's 27-year-old passing record, and at the end of the season, Sproles had 2,696 all-purpose yards, an NFL record.

"I had a lot of doubters in my first couple of years," Sproles says. "They always (said) that I'd be nothing more than a punt returner and a kick returner. So it felt good to get that record. It's always fun to prove people wrong. No matter what I do, people are going to say there's something that I can't do. I like showing them I can." And as his father Larry Sproles explained before Annette passed away: "You have to understand something. As an athlete, Darren takes after me. But as a person, Darren takes after his mother. They both will fight for what they believe in. And nobody will ever stop them."

Just like a tank.

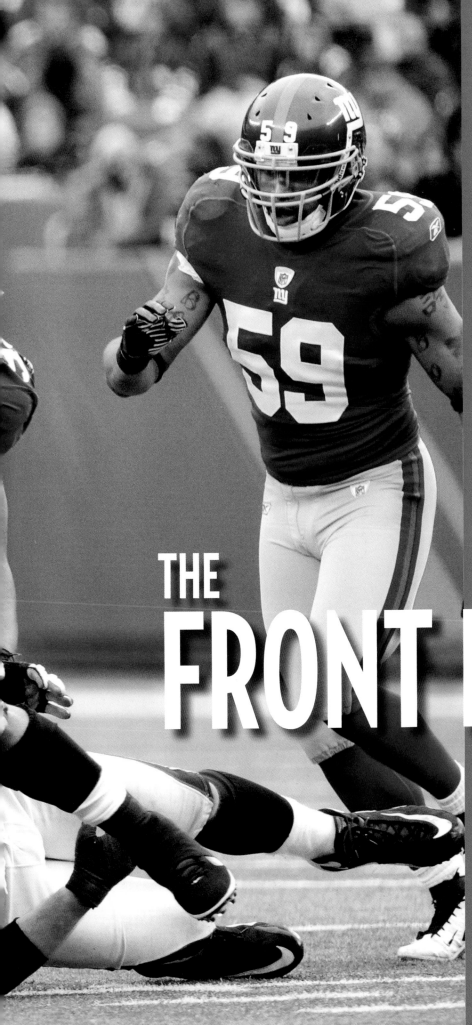

JARED ALLEN — Minnesota Vikings

DWIGHT FREENEY — Indianapolis Colts

JAKE LONG — Miami Dolphins

NICK MANGOLD — New York Jets

LOGAN MANKINS — New England Patriots

HALOTI NGATA — Baltimore Ravens

JULIUS PEPPERS — Chicago Bears

JASON PIERRE-PAUL — New York Giants

JUSTIN SMITH — San Francisco 49ers

NDAMUKONG SUH — Detroit Lions

JOE THOMAS — Cleveland Browns

JUSTIN TUCK — New York Giants

VINCE WILFORK — New England Patriots

THE
FRONT LINES

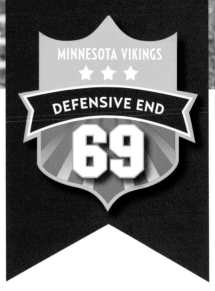

MINNESOTA VIKINGS
★ ★ ★

DEFENSIVE END

69

JARED ALLEN

In 2003, the Kansas City Chiefs won the AFC West with a 13–3 record and the best offense in the NFL. Their defense, however, was mediocre, a fact that was exposed by Peyton Manning and the Indianapolis Colts who handed the Chiefs a 31–28 loss in the first round of that season's playoffs. The Chiefs' defense needed help, and it came from a former calf-roper named Jared Allen.

Taken in the fourth round of the 2004 draft, Allen had nine

sacks in his rookie campaign, and while statistically the Chiefs' defense slipped that year, by 2007 they had one of the best defensive corps in the NFL and were first in preventing third-down conversions. Allen led the league with 15.5 sacks in 2007, but his impact on the NFL wasn't truly felt until the 2008 season.

Before the season, the Chiefs traded Allen to the Vikings for a first-round pick and two third-round picks. The void in Kansas was dramatic. The 2007 Chiefs with

Allen allowed 20.9 points per game, which, without Allen, was a stat that ballooned to 27.5 in 2008 and 26.5 in 2009, leaving the Chiefs 29th in the NFL during both years.

His impact on the fortunes of the Vikings franchise was put into perspective in two games played against the Green Bay Packers in 2009. The hype that season was focused on then Vikings quarterback and former Green Bay legend Brett Favre facing his old team, but Allen stole a share of the spotlight with 4.5

sacks in a 30–23 win and three more in a 38–26 victory, which carried Minnesota to the NFC North title.

Allen ended the season with 14.5 sacks versus the 10 that the entire Chiefs team had racked up, which is one of the reasons why, in 2010, Kerry J. Byrne of *Sports Illustrated* called Allen his "MV non-QB P" — Most Valuable non-quarterback Player — over the previous six seasons.

IN THE HUDDLE
Allen's website sells his *Quarterback Killers* cookbook and is home to the "Mullet Mullitia."

So why did K.C. give up such a valuable pass rusher in his prime? Two DUI charges in five months and subsequent jail time didn't help Allen's case, and after general manager Carl Peterson publicly called him "a young man at risk," Allen wanted out. To him, loyalty is paramount, and he felt betrayed after giving the organization everything he had. Allen made it clear to Peterson that he wouldn't re-sign when he became a free agent after the 2007 season, so instead of losing him for nothing, the Chiefs traded him.

Peterson's characterization of Allen wasn't entirely off-base. He was thrown out of high school for a stolen yearbook prank that cost him the chance to go to a big-name school that was courting him. He ended up at Idaho State University in Division I-AA, and while he was there he was arrested for battery, resisting arrest and a DUI, and he got thrown out of a game for punching an opponent in the face. On the other hand, he also won the Buck Buchanan Award for best defensive player in Division I-AA.

After being traded from Kansas City, Allen was determined to move on. He changed his diet, he stopped drinking and he began a mixed-martial-arts workout regimen. He's also an advocate for the Juvenile

Diabetes Research Foundation, as well as the founder of his own charitable foundation, Homes For Wounded Warriors, which builds accessible homes for disabled soldiers.

Allen solicits donations on his website, which also celebrates his love of hunting and his mullet. With an iPhone app, Twitter feed and Facebook page, not to mention a six-year, $72 million contract, Allen is every bit the modern athlete. Getting married, having a baby girl and taking USO trips to Kuwait and Iraq have also mellowed Allen, but fans know his fierceness on the field has not been affected. In a forgettable 2011 season for the Vikings as a whole, Allen finished half a sack shy of Michael Strahan's NFL sack record of 22.5 and was named Defensive Player of the Year. Allen's not playing for individual awards, though — he just wants back in the playoffs.

"In the playoffs it's like the business part of football is just

CAREER HIGHLIGHTS

- Four-time Pro Bowl selection (2007, 2008, 2009, 2011)
- Four-time All-Pro selection (2007, 2008, 2009, 2011)
- NFL Alumni Pass Rusher of the Year (2007)
- NFL Alumni Defensive Lineman of the Year (2009)
- NFL Defensive Player of the Year (2011)

gone," says Allen. "It isn't about how much money you make. Everybody makes the same amount [in the postseason]. It isn't about how good your team is, because every team is good. It's just, OK, are you going to kick my ass or am I going to kick your ass? It's a lot like the peewee football we used to play. Let's just go see who is better."

INDIANAPOLIS COLTS

★ ★ ★

DEFENSIVE END

93

DWIGHT FREENEY

CAREER HIGHLIGHTS

- Seven-time Pro Bowl selection (2003, 2004, 2005, 2008, 2009, 2010, 2011)

- Four-time All-Pro selection (2003, 2004, 2005, 2009)

- League-leading 16 sacks in 2004

- AFC Defensive Player of the Year (2005)

- Named to the NFL All-Decade Team for the 2000s

Dwight Freeney is unusual. From his route to quarterback, to his diet and recovery regime, to his feelings about former teammate Peyton Manning, Freeney takes the road a little less traveled.

Growing up in Bloomfield, Connecticut, Freeney was the son of Jamaican immigrants and was a soccer goalie who also lettered in high school baseball and basketball. It was the football coach, however, who wisely thought Freeney's size and speed might be better suited for the gridiron. Freeney earned a scholarship to Syracuse University playing defensive end and after two years as a starter, Freeney still holds the school records for sacks in a season (17.5) and a career (34).

Before he was drafted by the Indianapolis Colts with the 11th pick in the 2002 draft, Freeney was clocked at 4.38 seconds in the 40-yard dash and had a 40-inch vertical leap, which were impressive numbers for any player, let alone a defensive end. NFL scouts still wondered if Freeney was big enough to play the position, but the Colts' faith was rewarded immediately. Freeney was third in the league in sacks (13) in his rookie year, and he's since become the Colts'

all-time leader in the category, despite being repeatedly double– and triple-teamed. Freeney also led the league in 2004 with 16 sacks.

Freeney has two signature moves — one, for which he has been called "Corkscrew," to thwart the offensive line and the other to strip the quarterback. His 360-degree spin move which gave him his nickname is what gets him by his opponents, and his windmill chop is what he uses to strip the quarterback of the ball. Freeney learned the move by watching his childhood idol, Lawrence Taylor of the New York Giants, and while it was originally considered ineffective by conventional NFL wisdom, many young defensive ends are now coming into the league copying Freeney's twirling body and windmilling arms.

Freeney relies on his freakish speed to get him through, and he maintains his fitness with a regimented diet that, during the season, allows two cheat days a week (usually Monday and Tuesday). He sometimes gains five pounds over those two days, but the extra pounds are gone by Thursday with the help of food coach Leon Mellman, who ensures Freeney comes back to within a tenth of a pound of his ideal game weights. When he's preparing to play a pass-heavy offense, Freeney likes to weigh 262 pounds, and when he's up against a running team he prefers to weigh 267 pounds. Regardless of the opponent, Freeney drinks only grape juice, water and the occasional cup of tea, if he's treating himself. When going out to restaurants, Freeney brings his own ingredients and tells the chefs how to cook his meals. "I don't even take a chance with my toothpaste," says Freeney. "I stick with Crest."

This unique approach to staying in the game doesn't stop at the dining room table. Freeney's bedroom has a hyperbaric chamber and a portable infrared sauna, his kitchen has an Accelerated Recovery Performance (ARP) machine that sends electric currents through his muscles, his basement houses an inversion table he hangs upside down from for 15 minutes at a time and his home office has lasers that shoot beams of light into the cells of sore body parts.

"I know it's weird," admits Freeney. "Everything I do is weird. I ask myself all the time, 'What the hell am I doing?'"

IN THE HUDDLE
Freeney recovered a fumble and helped the Colts beat the Chicago Bears in Super Bowl XLI.

His relationship with quarterbacks, especially the former face of the Indianapolis franchise, is also a little odd. Freeney likes Peyton Manning as a person and recognized his value to the team, but, as Freeney opines, "He's a quarterback. I mean, imagine going through life like that — having everything so easy, being so soft, wearing a different-colored jersey in practice to symbolize you can't be touched. It pisses me off."

Before Manning and the Colts parted ways in 2012, Freeney would get particularly frustrated when facing Manning in training camp. "I'll come off the edge and a coach will scream, 'Don't touch the quarterback!' so I'll have to veer off, and it really burns me inside."

Freeney had said that if he and Manning played for separate teams that he would "have a giant picture of Peyton painted on the ceiling above [his] bed." Presumably, the work is being commissioned, and once it is done he'll surely stare at it from the comfort of his hyperbaric chamber.

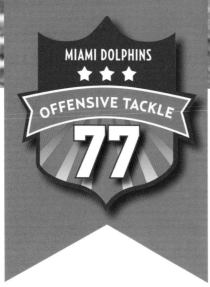

MIAMI DOLPHINS
★ ★ ★

OFFENSIVE TACKLE
77

JAKE LONG

When you have jumped out of your bedroom window from two stories up and then spent several days unconscious in the hospital as tubes do your breathing for you, facing adversity on the football field is put into perspective.

CAREER HIGHLIGHTS

- Two-time All-American (2006, 2007)
- Two-time Big Ten Offensive Lineman of the Year (2006, 2007)
- Four-time Pro Bowler (2008–11)
- Surrendered only 2.5 sacks in his rookie year (2008)

Jake Long had no choice but to jump early one June morning after his freshman year at the University of Michigan — fireworks lit up by his neighbors set his house on fire. The time, however, that Long spent in the hospital recuperating wouldn't be the only time he'd have to recover while at the University of Michigan; thankfully, no other incidents were nearly as dire or life-threatening.

An excellent high school baseball and basketball player in Laneer, Michigan, it was clear that Long was also destined to be a football player as he developed over 300 pounds of muscle and was the first player from his high school named to the All-State "Dream Team." A lifelong Wolverines fan, Long didn't spend much time debating his decision when Michigan recruited him.

Long spent his first year as a Wolverine as a redshirt freshman, and then started eight games in his sophomore season before undergoing shoulder surgery. In training camp the following year, he injured his ankle and missed another two months. A subsequent foot injury that season further limited Long's effectiveness.

Despite these setbacks, expectations were high for his junior year, and he arrived slimmed down from 338 pounds to 316.

The weight loss allowed him to be more effective in the Wolverines' new offensive system that relied on agility and quickness, and he was rewarded for his hard work being named an All-American for the 11–2 Wolverines.

IN THE HUDDLE
Long was the third offensive tackle ever taken first overall in the NFL draft, and fourth to be named to the Pro Bowl after his rookie year.

In recognition of his success and resilience, Long was named co-captain of the 2007 Wolverines in his senior season and his leadership was put to the test immediately when Michigan lost its opening game to Appalachian State in one of the biggest upsets in college football history. The team followed this loss by suffering their worst defeat since 1968, losing 39–7 to the University of Oregon in the second game of the season. Afterward, the ship was soon righted and the Wolverines won eight straight. At the end of the season, Long was an All-American again, and was named Big Ten Offensive Lineman of the Year and a finalist for the Outland Trophy. He was also praised by his coaches and teammates for his fortitude and poise, characteristics that were not lost on the Miami Dolphins.

After working out a deal before the draft, Miami took Long first overall, making him only the third offensive tackle to ever be the top pick, after Orlando Pace in 1997 and Hall of Famer Ron Yary in 1968. Long's five-year, $57.75 million-dollar deal made him (at the time) the highest paid offensive lineman in NFL history.

Long is often compared to the Cleveland Browns' Joe Thomas, who overtook Long as the highest paid offensive lineman before the 2011 season. The two tackles were a year apart in the draft (Thomas went third overall the year before Long was drafted) and usually appear in rankings as the league's top two left tackles.

According to Tim Graham of ESPN, "Choosing between Long and Thomas is splitting hairs. They've been selected for the Pro Bowl every season [they have been] in the NFL and are the reigning first-team All-Pros. Thomas was the third overall draft pick in 2007, Long the top choice in 2008. But I [give] Long the edge because of the circumstances he has dealt with in Miami."

Those circumstances include a three-season plunge that saw the Miami Dolphins go from an 11–5 record and the AFC East title in Long's rookie season of 2008 (a 10-win improvement from their dreadful 1–15 record in 2007), to finishing the next two years at 7–9; in 2011, the Dolphins bottomed out with a 6–10 record.

Despite these losing records, Long has never missed a game and has played in the Pro Bowl after each season, becoming just the fourth first overall pick to make it to the Pro Bowl after his rookie year. In 2010, when the Pro Bowl was played in Miami, Long was the lone Dolphins representative.

With Reggie Bush showing signs of being the back that many projected he would be when he was selected second overall by the New Orleans Saints in 2006, Long will continue to protect and guide the way for his Dolphins teammates. Besides, after leaping from a burning building, leading the Dolphins back to the playoffs shouldn't seem like such a daunting task.

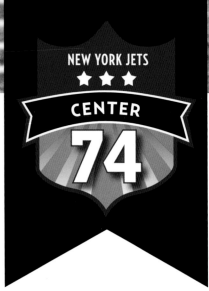

NICK MANGOLD

The center might be the hardest-worked position in football; the player snaps the ball on virtually every play and then almost instantaneously has to block a 300-pound opponent (or two) so the recipient of the snap isn't crushed and so a running back has a path down the field. As these crucial plays are repeated over and over again, a synergy develops between the center and the quarterback, with the latter owing much of their success — and ability to walk off the field — to the former.

New York Jets center Nick Mangold is generally considered the best in the NFL at his position, which is fitting for a man from Centerville, Ohio, where he was a first-team All-State selection while playing both offense and defense for Archbishop Alter High School.

Later, at Ohio State University, Mangold was a co-captain in his senior season and was an Outland Trophy finalist for best interior lineman after not allowing a sack the entire year and helping the Buckeyes generate 5,068 yards of offense, an average of more than 422 yards per game.

Drafted 29th overall in 2006, Mangold was the first center in Jets history to start every game in his first year. Tackle D'Brickashaw Ferguson was drafted fourth that same year, and it was the first time since 1975 that a team took two offensive linemen in the first round. Together, Mangold and Ferguson are the only two offensive linemen in NFL

history to start the first 75 games of their careers together.

In 2009, as the Jets set a team record for rushing yards, Mangold made his first All-Pro team and second Pro Bowl. Following these accomplishments (and leading up to the 2010 season), Mangold was due for a raise, and even though negotiations dragged, in the end the Jets recognized the value of their star center. His chemistry with the Jets' quarterback of the future, Mark Sanchez, who was drafted in 2009, was enough for the club to make Mangold the highest paid center in the league.

The dynamic duo of Mangold and Sanchez led the Jets to back-to-back trips to the AFC Championship game in 2009 and 2010, but in 2011, Mangold missed the first two games of his career with a high ankle sprain. The Jets didn't make the playoffs and ended the season with an 8–8 record. Much of the blame fell on the shoulders of Sanchez.

IN THE HUDDLE

Mangold joined Jets owner Robert W. Johnson IV to commission the USS *New York*, which was built with steel from the World Trade Center.

Mangold defended the shots: "I know the guy had a rough go about it," he said after the season was over. "As an offensive line, in our group, we did not do the things to put him in a position to win. We did not protect him as well as we should

have; we did not run the ball as well as we should have. Unfortunately, he kind of takes the brunt of the criticism, even though we share in that blame … we should be taking most of it."

With the addition of quarterback Tim Tebow — the center of attention for much of the 2011 season — Mangold became even more valuable to the Jets as Tebow provides the team with a wildcat option to help support the newly re-signed Sanchez.

But if there's one man who can handle the multitasking, it's Mangold, and he will have to balance the different styles and

talents of Tebow and Sanchez while protecting them from the New York media hounds and the inevitable quarterback controversy they will create.

Mangold, however, isn't the only one carrying a load in 2012. His sister, Holley, who made headlines in 2006 when she became the first female in Ohio to play offensive line in high school, is an Olympic weightlifter in the super-heavyweight division.

With a son in the NFL and a daughter who finished 10th in London at her first Olympics, the Mangold family has had quite a year, and according to their father Vern, that's "pretty heavy."

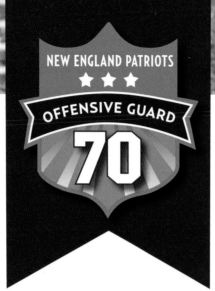

LOGAN MANKINS

Offensive linemen are integral to a team's success but are generally anonymous to the casual NFL observer. Some, however, by virtue of their play and personality, manage to shine though. Logan Mankins is one such person.

Mankins grew up on a 10,000-acre farm in Catheys Valley, California, and dreamed of making a name for himself as a steer roper. This dream didn't come true, but his roping skills have been put to good use as an offensive guard for the New England Patriots, with whom he uses leverage, strength and proper technique to protect his teammates from the animals on the other side of the line.

At Fresno State University, Mankins didn't allow a sack or a quarterback pressure his entire senior season, and his blocks sprung his teammates to 16 touchdowns. He was also named All-Western Athletic Conference, was the first offensive lineman to win the team's MVP award and was rated the top offensive guard prospect in the country by the NFL Draft Report, even though he was a tackle in college.

The Patriots obviously agreed with popular opinion — they drafted Mankins with the final pick of the first round in 2005 and started him at left guard in every game that year (he was the first Patriots rookie guard since 1973 to do so).

CAREER HIGHLIGHTS

- Four-time All-Pro selection (2007, 2009–2011)

- Four-time Pro Bowl selection (2007, 2009–2011)

- Leader of a New England offense that has ranked in the top 10 in five of Mankins' six seasons with the team

- All-American Dream Team selection

- Rated the best offensive guard prospect in college football by the NFL Draft Report during his senior college season

- First offensive lineman to be named MVP of the Fresno State Bulldogs

In 2007, Mankins made his first All-Pro and Pro Bowl teams after helping Tom Brady set a record 50 touchdown passes and assisting the Patriots in becoming the highest-scoring team in NFL history; they finished the regular season undefeated.

Mankins and the offensive line were even more important the following season when Brady went down in the first game of 2008 with torn ligaments in his knee and was lost for the year. With Brady out, the Patriots relied on their ground game, and they finished the season ranked fifth in the NFL in offense thanks, in large part, to their running game, which posted 20-year franchise highs in rushing yards, rushing touchdowns and yards per carry.

In 2011, Mankins was essential again as he helped the Patriots achieve a record-breaking offensive season — his work at guard enabled Brady to throw for the second-most yards in NFL history, and many of his passes were caught by tight end Rob Gronkowski, who in his rookie year set the NFL touchdown record for the position. Further, without Mankins, Randy Moss might not be the NFL's single-season touchdown

record-holder (23 in 2007) and Wes Welker might still be a marginal player instead of a three-time NFL receptions leader (112 in 2007, 123 in 2009 and 122 in 2011). The team's offensive line played a huge role in these players' achievements, and Mankins was the leader of the group as well as its best player. He had earned the right to be paid accordingly by the time his rookie contract came to a close.

IN THE HUDDLE

Mankins scored his first and only career touchdown in the 2006 AFC Championship game when he recovered a fumble in the end zone, giving the Patriots a 7–0 lead against the Indianapolis Colts.

Negotiations were contentious, and the Patriots designated Mankins as their franchise player, blocking teams from signing him as a free agent while New England management continued to bargain. Mankins wasn't happy about it.

"Right now, this is about principle with me and keeping your word and how you treat people … Growing up, I was taught a man's word is his bond. Obviously this isn't

the case with the Patriots."

Mankins felt as if the Patriots had broken a promise when they didn't sign him to a contract extension, so he held out for the first seven games of the 2010 season. He only played nine games that year, but he still made the All-Pro and Pro Bowl teams, and on the eve of the 2011 season, he signed a six-year, $51 million contract that included a $20 million signing bonus.

Holding strong to his principles also led Mankins to later file an antitrust suit against the NFL. Along with nine other players (including Brady), Mankins launched the suit as part of the complicated labor negotiations between the players' union and team owners that threatened to derail the 2011 season. Eventually, however, the owners and players came to an 11th-hour agreement that ensured football peace for the next decade.

Now that Mankins' off-the-field issues are taken care of and he is signed through 2016, he can chase the elusive Vince Lombardi Trophy, and if he can rope it in he won't just stand alongside Brady as teammate, superstar and shrewd negotiator, he'll also be a Super Bowl champion.

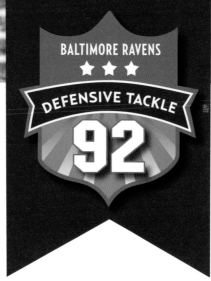

BALTIMORE RAVENS
★ ★ ★
DEFENSIVE TACKLE
92

HALOTI NGATA

E tuini Haloti Ngata, better known as Haloti Ngata (pronounced "ha-LOW-tee NAHtah") was named after his uncle, which is a family custom in Tonga, where Ngata's parents, Solomone and Olga, emigrated from before Ngata was born.

"It's a respect thing in our culture," says Ngata, whose four siblings are also named after relatives. "Family is everything to us, and this is just one way we acknowledge that."

Ngata was born in Inglewood, California, but went to Highland

High School, in Salt Lake City, Utah, after his family relocated there. It was here that Ngata was named Utah Player of the Year in 2001 and topped several lists as the top defensive player and interior lineman in the country.

After considering attending

Brigham Young University, Ngata, a devout Mormon, decided to go to the University of Oregon, where he was a unanimous All-American, as well as a finalist for both the Outland Trophy and the Bronko Nagurski Award as a junior.

Sadly, Ngata lost both of his parents before they could enjoy his success in the NFL. During Ngata's freshman year at Oregon, his father died when his work truck slid off an icy road, and then, just after Ngata's junior season, his mother died of complications from diabetes.

IN THE HUDDLE

Since Ngata entered the NFL, the Ravens have allowed a league-low 41 rushing touchdowns, the NFL's fewest rushing first downs (420), and the team has ranked in the top five in run defense each season.

Ngata's mother's health played a major factor in his decision to enter the NFL draft a year early. He had first considered leaving school to take care of her, but thought playing professionally would do the most to help the situation, so he asked for her blessing. She agreed 12 days before passing away.

Three days after her funeral, Ngata went to Houston with his namesake uncle to prepare for the draft.

"This had always been his dream, and he wanted to follow through on it, especially because his mother had supported it," says Haloti Moala, Ngata's uncle. "He wanted to make sure he was in the best shape he could be for the combine. Football kept him going when his father died, and it's done the same for him through his mother's death."

Ngata continues to honor his parents by being as hardworking and diligent as they were and by

carrying on Tongan traditions. One of his customs has a practical application — Ngata practices the "Haka" traditional war dance to hone his balance, footwork and swift motions.

"For me, the Haka is calling upon my ancestors to have their spirits with me on the field," says Ngata. "It's great. It's wonderful. I love doing it. It makes me feel closer to my culture."

Ngata ended up signing with the Baltimore Ravens, who traded up to select him 12th overall in 2006, and now, as one of the NFL's most athletic defensive tackles, the 6-foot-4, 330-pound Ngata stops the run (393 career tackles), rushes the passer (17 career sacks) and even covers receivers (3 career interceptions).

In 2011, Ngata led the NFL's third-ranked defense (which was second against the run and best in the league in the red zone) with 64 tackles, 5 sacks for a loss of 21 yards, 3 fumble recoveries — including his first for a touchdown — and 2 forced fumbles.

Further, in two postseason games in 2011, Ngata had six tackles, one pass deflection and one forced fumble, and the Ravens' stout defense frazzled Tom Brady and the New England Patriots in the AFC Championship game, in which Baltimore came within a missed field goal of reaching the Super Bowl. It was the second time in Ngata's career that he was one game away from the big dance.

Green Bay Packers center Jeff Saturday thinks Ngata is the NFL's best defensive tackle: "This is the guy that I wouldn't want to be facing if the game is on the line. I think Haloti could play free safety; he's got that kind of athletic ability. And when he lines up, he'll play off the ball somewhat and in a flex position. He will bring all 340 pounds to you. He's an absolute monster." And before the 2011 season even began, the Ravens paid

CAREER HIGHLIGHTS

• Four-time Pro Bowl selection (2008–2011)

• Four-time All-Pro (2008–2011)

• All-Rookie Team (2006)

• Consensus All-American at the University of Oregon (2005)

• Utah Player of the Year (2001)

Ngata as such, signing him to a five-year, $61 million contract. In doing so, Baltimore is showing it knows legendary mainstays Ray Lewis and Ed Reed won't be with the team forever, and is building the future of its defense around players like Ngata and Terrell Suggs.

In the meantime, Lewis, Reed, Suggs and Ngata will continue to terrorize the league, with Ngata leading the way, right down the middle.

JULIUS PEPPERS

Julius Frazier Peppers was seemingly born to play on the hardcourt. Named after two of the best basketball players of all time — Julius Erving and Walt Frazier — and over six-feet-tall before he hit high school, Peppers was literally head and shoulders above everyone else at Southern Nash High School in Bailey, North Carolina.

His size and athletic ability were so great they earned him many nicknames, most notably "Big Head" for his hat size and "Freak of Nature" for his seemingly otherworldly ability.

"I've known Julius since the fifth grade," says Alton Tyre, his high school track coach. "I was in Wilmington when Michael Jordan was there. I coached against Clyde Simmons. Julius is the greatest athlete I have ever seen. A guy that big and that strong is not supposed to be that fast."

Basketball was the 6-foot-7 Peppers' first love, and by the end of his career at Southern Nash he had more than 1,600 points, 800 rebounds and 200 assists, and was heavily recruited by legendary Duke University coach Mike Krzyzewski. Peppers, however, chose to go to the University of North Carolina and become a Tar Heel who played both football and basketball.

Peppers continued to gain notoriety as he helped his basketball team reach the 2000 Final Four, and he further marked his territory on the football field by leading the country with 15 sacks in his sophomore season, which was a total one shy of NFL Hall of Famer Lawrence Taylor's school record. In Peppers' junior year, his final season, he decided his future was in football and gave up his hoop dreams to better focus on the gridiron.

It paid off. Peppers won the Rotary Lombardi Award and Chuck Bednarik Award, and he left the school second in Tar Heels history with 30.5 sacks before becoming the Carolina Panthers' first selection, second overall (the highest pick in franchise history), in the 2002 draft.

In eight seasons with the

CAREER HIGHLIGHTS

- Seven-time Pro Bowl selection (2004–2006, 2008–2011)

- Five-time All-Pro (2004, 2006, 2008–2010)

- NFL All-Decade Team for the 2000s

- NFC Defensive Player of the Year and NFL Alumni Lineman of the Year (2004)

- Defensive Rookie of the Year (2002)

- First-team All-American and Winner of the Rotary Lombardi Award (for best college lineman) and Chuck Bednarik Award (for best defensive player) as a junior at the University of North Carolina (2001)

Panthers, Peppers became the team's all-time leader in sacks, forced fumbles and blocked kicks, as well as one of only eight players in NFL history with double-digit sacks in four of his first five seasons. But, the hometown hero eventually had to leave, and when Peppers became an unrestricted free agent after the 2009 season, the Chicago Bears outbid everyone with a six-year, $91.5 million contract.

"It was time for a change, not only from that franchise but from the state," says Peppers. "I'm from a small town, and I've lived in Charlotte, which is really a small city and a small town too, but I've never lived in a big city or had to perform under the spotlight in one. That's a challenge in itself."

Some questioned the Bears' investment because the knock on Peppers was that he wasn't a passionate player and he didn't get the most out of his prodigious talent. Former and current teammates disagree. "I never saw the kid take a practice off," says quarterback Jake Delhomme, Peppers' teammate in Carolina for seven seasons. "I never saw him miss a practice in training camp. I never saw him miss practice during the season. I never saw him gloat. He came to play, he came to work. Julius is a quiet guy, and people might misunderstand him because he keeps to himself."

IN THE HUDDLE

In his rookie season, Peppers was suspended for the final four games after testing positive for ephedra, which he said came from a dietary supplement. No matter — he still won Defensive Rookie of the Year with 12 sacks in 12 games.

Chicago Bear Israel Idonije agrees: "I think it starts with his character — who he is off the field and what he brings as a leader and his work [ethic]. It correlates directly to performance. Focus, every snap — 100 percent."

Peppers was always thoughtful and unassuming, even as he dominated every sport he tried. His mother, Bessie, who raised him as a single parent, made sure of it. Once, at halftime of a high school basketball game she made him spit out his gum because she thought it looked like he was showboating.

Indeed, Peppers is not one to show up his opponents or gloat in their faces. On the final day of the 2011 regular season, he had his 11th sack, which was the seventh time in 10 years he achieved a double-digit total and which was a feat that put him in elite company with 100 career sacks. After that play, he simply walked back to the line of scrimmage for third down.

And after the season, the hardworking superstar quietly got on a plane to Hawaii and headed to his seventh Pro Bowl.

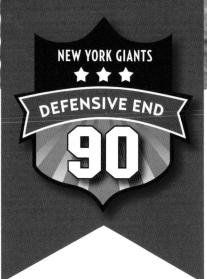

NEW YORK GIANTS
DEFENSIVE END
90

JASON PIERRE-PAUL

Jason Pierre-Paul is a football neophyte, and that should scare the heck out of New York Giants opponents because if he's already dominant after only six years of football, how difficult will it be to contain him once he has the sport figured out?

Pierre-Paul was the third of five children growing up in Deerfield Beach, Florida, where his parents settled after emigrating from Haiti. After settling in the U.S., his mother, Marie, worked 12-hour days to take care of the family because his father, Jean, had lost his vision when Jason was a one year old. Marie became protective of her son after he broke his leg playing basketball, so when he decided to play football he kept her from worry by telling his mom he was staying late at school to do homework.

He had actually joined the team at the suggestion of his geometry teacher, who also happened to be the team's defensive coordinator. "If he wanted to pass the class," says Manny Martin, who played defensive back for the Houston Oilers and Buffalo Bills, "I strongly encouraged him to play."

As a junior just starting out in the sport of football, Pierre-Paul didn't get much field time, but he was a quick study and as a senior he was a wrecking ball who caught the eyes of major college recruiters. Unfortunately, Pierre-Paul didn't qualify academically for a scholarship, so he went the junior college route instead. He played for two schools in two years until Kevin Patrick, the defensive line coach at the University of South Florida who had always kept tabs on the locally raised Pierre-Paul, brought him to the team two weeks before their season opener in 2009. It didn't take long for Pierre-Paul to start appearing on the draft radar, but it was still a bit of a surprise when the Giants chose him 15th overall in 2010. "He came from nowhere," said Hall of Fame quarterback and ESPN draft analyst Steve Young.

IN THE HUDDLE
Super Bowl XLVI was the first time Jean Pierre-Paul attended one of his son's games; Pierre-Paul credits his father for inspiring his relentless drive on the field.

Pierre-Paul's first season in the NFL was decent but not spectacular, and some were already starting to call him a first-round bust. Naysayers ate their words in 2011, when, after a year's apprenticeship, Pierre-Paul proved he had arrived during a nationally televised game against division rival and sworn enemy the Dallas Cowboys.

The first of Pierre-Paul's team-high eight tackles in the game

knocked Cowboys quarterback Tony Romo into his own end zone for a safety that put New York up 2–0, and as the first half wound down, "JPP" stripped the ball from running back Felix Jones to set up a go-ahead field goal. In the third quarter, Pierre-Paul sacked Romo again, and in the fourth quarter he finished the signature game of his blossoming career by blocking Dan Bailey's 47-yard field-goal attempt with one second remaining. Pierre-Paul single-handedly caused an eight-point swing in the 37–34 victory that ended a four-game losing streak for the Giants and started their spectacular run to the playoffs.

"Jason Pierre-Paul, if you're not in the Pro Bowl this year, there should be an investigation," said NBC color commentator Cris Collinsworth.

There was no need to go to such lengths — Pierre-Paul was named to the Pro Bowl as well as named a first-team All-Pro. His 16.5 sacks were the most by a Giant since Michael Strahan's 18.5 in 2003, his 29 quarterback hits were 19 higher than any other teammate's and his 23 tackles for losses were 10 more than any other Giant in 2011.

Pierre-Paul, in what surely must be a first, had never even watched a Super Bowl before playing in one. A reporter suggested to him that a second-year player might be nervous facing a player like Tom Brady in a game watched by over 100 million Americans.

"Me not knowing anything about my opponents is a great thing," he said. "I just play."

That simple method seemed to work for Pierre-Paul — he deflected two passes and helped the Giants hold Brady in check for most of the game, including during the last

CAREER HIGHLIGHTS

- Named to the Pro Bowl (2011)
- First-team All-Pro (2011)
- NFC Defensive Player of the Month (December 2011)
- Two-time NFC Defensive Player of the Week (2011)
- Super Bowl XLVI champion

minute when the Patriots were driving for the win.

With the Giants' 21–17 victory in Super Bowl XLVI, Pierre-Paul capped a season for the ages, and with his best football years yet to come, this probably won't be the last time he has his hands on the Lombardi Trophy. "I'm still learning," he said. "I'm taking steps. I have a ways to go."

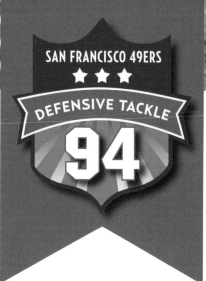

SAN FRANCISCO 49ERS
★ ★ ★

DEFENSIVE TACKLE

94

JUSTIN SMITH

CAREER HIGHLIGHTS

- Three-time Pro Bowl selection (2009, 2010, 2011)

- All-Pro selection in 2011 (both first and second teams)

- Named Defensive Player of the Year by *Sports Illustrated's* Peter King

- First team All-American (2000)

- Two-time All-Big 12 (1999, 2000)

Justin Smith is an overnight success 11 years in the making. The culmination of his hard work came in the 2011 season when the San Francisco 49ers' defensive tackle and defensive end had a coming-out party after making several jaw-dropping plays while anchoring one of the stingiest defenses in the NFL. Smith's adulations had finally arrived after a decade of playing quietly dominant football.

At 61.0 rushing yards allowed per game in 2011 (which was 21.5 less than the second-place Houston Texans and 50 fewer than the Super Bowl champion New York Giants), the 49ers allowed the fewest rushing yards in the league. Smith was integral to their success and for the first time was voted an All-Pro — twice. He was placed on the team at both of his positions, which was the first time in history anyone had achieved such a feat.

Defensive tackles tend to cede the spotlight to higher-profile positions, but a few individual plays created a reluctant star out of Smith in the 2011 season. In a game against the Philadelphia Eagles, the 6-foot-4, 285-pound Smith chased down fleet-footed receiver Jeremy Maclin and stripped the ball from him, securing a come-from-behind win. In another game against the Giants, Smith leapt over the scrum late in the fourth quarter to bat down an Eli Manning pass, once again ensuring a victory. His biggest play of all, however, occurred in the playoffs when he pushed back the New Orleans Saints' Jermon Bushrod like he was a tackling dummy and then reached over him to grab quarterback Drew Brees. It was yet another momentum-stealing play in the fourth quarter, and one that sent the 49ers to the NFC Championship.

IN THE HUDDLE

After receiving enough votes as both defensive tackle and defensive end (he switches positions depending on formation), Smith was named to the first *and* second All-Pro teams after the 2011 season, which was the first time a player had ever received this honor.

In light of these accomplishments, it's not a surprise that the man who is called "Cowboy" (for his Midwestern roots and work ethic) excels as the game wears on. Throughout his career, Smith hasn't missed a game due to injury and he is on the field for over 90 percent of the 49ers' defensive plays.

"I don't think there is a tougher player that I've ever been around or known," says head coach Jim Harbaugh. "I was talking with

[defensive coaches] about the same thing. Do you know a tougher guy than Justin Smith? Have you ever been around a player like this? We really couldn't come up with one."

The team was hoping for this kind of player when they wooed Smith as a free agent in 2008 with a helicopter ride over downtown San Francisco and Alcatraz. However, the country boy from Holts Summit, Missouri, was more interested in what the 49ers were building, and he signed on to become part of that future.

In the four seasons Smith has been in San Francisco, he has led the team with 29.0 sacks (the most of any defensive tackle in the league over those four seasons) and he's already second in franchise history for sacks at the position.

Smith had previously been toiling away in anonymity with the Cincinnati Bengals after they had drafted him fourth overall out of the University of Missouri in 2001. While in Cincinnati, he appeared in only one playoff game, which was a first-round loss to the Pittsburgh Steelers following the 2005 season.

Now, however, Smith is being individually recognized as a major contributor to the 49ers' success, in part because his work ethic is rubbing off on teammate Aldon Smith.

Aldon is also from Missouri, and in 2009, he broke — by half a sack — Justin's 2001 school sack record at their alma mater. The Smiths now sit two lockers apart, and Justin spent the lockout prior to the 2011 season helping Aldon

prepare for his rookie campaign after he was picked seventh overall. Their efforts paid off — in 2011, Aldon led the team in sacks, with 14, which was half a sack shy of the NFL rookie record.

"They've worked well together," says Vic Fangio, the 49ers' defensive coordinator. "They've kind of had a good relationship of big brother/little brother, and I think Aldon has been able to elevate his game because he's seen how much toughness and tenacity enters into this equation."

In 2012, the NFL will forget the Joneses because everyone is going to spend their time keeping up with the Smiths — including a third, quarterback Alex Smith — or else risk being flattened on the road to New Orleans for Super Bowl XLVII.

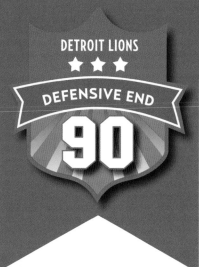

NDAMUKONG SUH

Ndamukong (en-DOM-ah-ken), which means "House of Spears" in Cameroon's Gema tribe, is an imposing name on its own. Attributed to a defensive tackle who's 6-foot-4 and over 300 pounds, and it's downright intimidating.

Growing up in Portland, Oregon, Ndamukong Suh was a prolific soccer player. As a kid, he threw his considerable weight around and kicked the ball with such ferocity that his mother, Bernadette, had to carry around his birth certificate to prove he was the same age as his opponents.

Because of his size, it was only a matter of time before the football field beckoned, and after dominating on his high school's offensive and defensive lines, Suh went to the University of Nebraska, where he became a Cornhusker legend by winning just about every defensive award imaginable and finishing fourth in Heisman voting as a senior.

The Detroit Lions, by virtue of another forgettable season, took Suh with the second overall pick in the 2010 draft, and in his first season he had 10 sacks, won the Defensive Rookie of the Year Award and was named to the Pro Bowl and All-Pro teams. He was also heavily fined for his aggressive play.

"The problem with the league is, they've never seen a defensive tackle like this," explains Detroit's defensive coordinator Gunther Cunningham. "He's the best football player at that position I've ever seen."

In just one season, Suh became the face of the Lions' defense, and, by helping replace a local high school football team's equipment after it was stolen, a public figure in Detroit.

"For him to take the time to do that meant a lot to those young men," says Tyrone Winfrey, president of the Detroit Board of Education. "When I look at Detroit and the shots we've taken with crime and unemployment, to have the Lions and Tigers winning, we are truly grateful. And to have a positive role model like Ndamukong Suh come to our city, I'm excited about the young people who will be impacted by his success."

Therein lies the dichotomy of Suh — he engenders goodwill and respect off the field, yet on it he has been known to play outside the lines. In one of the most-watched games this side of the Super Bowl (the traditional Thanksgiving Day game between the Lions and the Green Bay Packers), Suh was capable of shoving Packers guard Evan Dietrich-Smith's head into the turf after the play was over and then, as Dietrich-Smith righted himself, he stomped on his arm for good measure.

After the game, Suh said he was simply trying to catch his balance, but the league didn't buy it and he was suspended for two games without pay.

The stomp had repercussions beyond Suh's playing time and his wallet: The high-profile Thanksgiving Day game had relevance for the first time in years because the Lions were fighting for divisional supremacy with the Packers; Suh, after having topped a Nielsen-EPoll survey of the most-liked NFL players in September was voted in a December Forbes magazine poll as one of the most disliked athletes in America. "He went from being so popular to being a pariah in one season," says Stephen Master, vice president, Head of Sports, for Nielsen.

Suh eventually apologized for his actions. "Playing professional sports is not a game," he said on his Facebook page. "It is a profession with great responsibility, and where

CAREER HIGHLIGHTS

- All-Pro and Pro Bowl selection (2010)
- Named Defensive Rookie of the Year (2010)
- Associated Press College Player of the Year (2009)
- Unanimous All-American selection (2009)

performance on and off the field should never be compromised. It requires a calm and determined demeanor, which cannot be derailed by the game, referee calls, fans or other players."

If Suh lives by those words, he should be able to swing the pendulum of public opinion back his way while still helping his team restore its roar. Besides, after their 2011 playoff appearance — their first in 12 years, a 45–28 loss in the first round to the New Orleans Saints — the young Lions have a tremendous future ahead of them. Pride is being restored in Detroit and a deep playoff run would put an end to the slings and arrows being aimed at the city, the team and the man.

CLEVELAND BROWNS
★ ★ ★
OFFENSIVE TACKLE
73

JOE THOMAS

On draft day in 2007, Cleveland Browns fans were dreaming of a hotshot riding in from the University of Notre Dame to reverse their waning fortunes. They were convinced the Browns would make Brady Quinn the third overall pick and he would become an elite, championship-caliber quarterback, the way fellow Fighting Irish alumni Joe Montana and Joe Theismann had. Instead they got Joe Thomas, a tackle from the University of Wisconsin, who was out fishing with his dad when his name was called.

During high school, Thomas was a "Joe" of all trades, playing right tackle, defensive end, tight end, fullback, placekicker and punter. He was heavily recruited as an offensive lineman by Notre Dame, the Univeristy of Michigan, Ohio State and the University of Nebraska before he decided to stay in his home state and play for Wisconsin, first as a blocking tight end and then as a left tackle.

Thomas was a starter from day one, and as a Badger he cleared the path for running backs Brian Calhoun and P.J. Hill Jr., who both had career years that season, gaining over 1,500 yards before fading into obscurity.

At the end of Thomas' junior year in 2006, he considered declaring for the NFL draft, where he was projected to be a top-15 pick, but at the end of that season, Wisconsin was playing in the Capital One Bowl and was in need of help on the defense. Proving his versatility and commitment to the team, Thomas filled a hole at

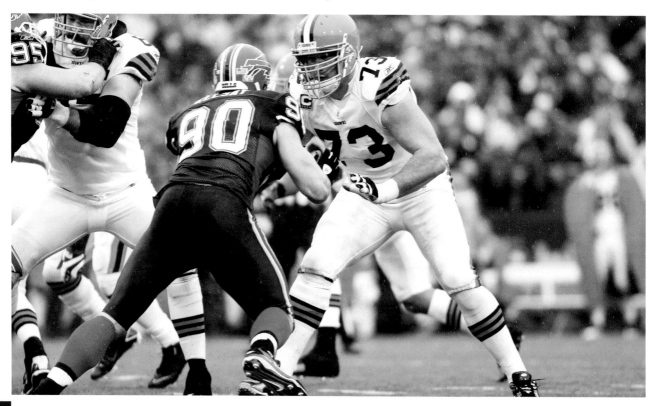

defensive end. Out of his normal position, he tore his ACL and his NFL dream took a serious hit.

Returning to Wisconsin for his senior year, it was clear Thomas' injury didn't have any lasting effects. He was named a consensus All-American player and won the Outland Trophy as the nation's top lineman. Wisconsin won the Capital One Bowl that season, ended the year with a 12–1 record — a school high for wins in a season — and ranked seventh in the country.

However, Thomas' senior season was touched by tradegy. High school friend and ex-teammate Luke Homan disappeared, and when Thomas heard the news, he rushed to join the search party. By the time Thomas arrived, Homan's body had been found in the Mississippi River.

IN THE HUDDLE
Thomas cohosts *Outdoors Ohio with D'Arcy Egan & Joe Thomas* on Sports Time Ohio.

"Joe joined the search for his friend because Joe cares deeply about his family and those close to him," says Bret Bielema, Thomas' head coach in his senior season at Wisconsin. "He knew he wanted to do whatever he could to help find Luke and he wanted to be there to comfort Luke's family and friends. Again, it speaks to Joe's character."

That character and personality fit Ohio's blue-collar work ethic perfectly, and Thomas' success on the field with the Browns has only improved his stature in Cleveland. He came second in Rookie of the Year voting after playing every down, and was the only player not named Adrian Peterson to receive even a single a vote, as Peterson won in a landslide.

Since 2006, Thomas' knee — and the rest of his 6-foot-6, 312-pound body — have held up against the grueling trench warfare of the NFL, and he has yet to miss a game

in his five-year career. He has also been named to the Pro Bowl after every season he's played, and has been selected as a first-team All-Pro three times.

As a left tackle, Thomas has protected a carousel of Cleveland quarterbacks, as well as running back Peyton Hillis, who can thank Thomas for opening the holes that led to his breakthrough 2010 season that landed Hillis on the cover of EA Sports' Madden NFL 12 in 2011.

The Browns have wisely decided to make Thomas the anchor of their offensive line in the years to come, and the big left tackle showed his loyalty by signing a six-year, $43 million contract before the start of the 2011 season. Had Thomas become a free agent in 2012, he probably would have been wooed by about 31 other teams, and Cleveland

CAREER HIGHLIGHTS
- Named to the Pro Bowl five times (2007–11), becoming the second Cleveland Brown, after Hall of Fame running back Jim Brown, to be selected after each of his first five seasons.
- Three-time first team All-Pro (2009–11)
- Second team All-Pro (2008)

might have lost one of their few marquee players as well as the team's working-class hero — not only has Thomas never missed a game, he's never even missed a practice.

While the fans in the Browns' Dawg Pound may have had their reservations at the 2007 draft, Thomas has proven that he's no Average Joe.

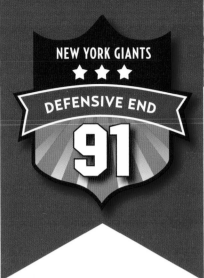

NEW YORK GIANTS
★ ★ ★

DEFENSIVE END

91

JUSTIN TUCK

CAREER HIGHLIGHTS

- Two-time Pro Bowl selection (2008, 2010)

- Two-time All-Pro selection (2008, 2010)

- Two-time Super Bowl champion (XLII, XLVI)

- Set the Notre Dame single-season and career sack records (13.5 and 24.5, respectively), as well as the record for career stops behind the line of scrimmage (43)

During the bye week of the New York Giants' 2011 season, director of player development Charles Way invited fighter pilots to the team facility to explain the importance of debriefing sessions, in which pilots returning from missions build trust by openly discussing the mistakes they made. In these meetings, rank is irrelevant and candor is encouraged. Giants defensive end Justin Tuck took up the cause and after every game leads a debriefing session for the team's defense.

He wasn't always the top dog — growing up in Kellyton, Alabama, Tuck had five older sisters who "bossed him around." It wasn't long, though, before he outgrew them, sprouting to 6-foot-5 and becoming a star on the basketball court. When he took up football, he played quarterback, eventually switching to tight end and defensive end and earning the 2000 Alabama Class 4A Player of the Year award.

Tuck chose to go to the University of Notre Dame but had to sit out his freshman year with injuries, and then played only sparingly in his sophomore season. After months of sitting out with pent-up energy, Tuck broke out in his junior year, set the Fighting Irish record for sacks in a season (13.5), and by the time he graduated, also held the career record of 24.5.

After being chosen by the Giants in the third round of the 2005 draft,

Tuck had a slow start to his NFL career, as he was stuck behind Pro Bowlers Michael Strahan and Osi Umenyiora on the depth chart. Two years later, in 2007, Tuck came out of the shadows and had 10 sacks, 65 tackles and 2 forced fumbles — all despite starting only two games.

If this wasn't enough to convince the Giants of Tuck's abilities, his work in the playoffs sealed the deal. After winning three road games to reach Super Bowl XLII, the Giants weren't given much of a chance against the previously undefeated New England Patriots and their all-world quarterback Tom Brady.

IN THE HUDDLE

Tuck wrote a children's book based on his childhood in Alabama. It is called *Home-Field Advantage* and was published in support of his R.U.S.H. (Read, Understand, Succeed, Hope) for Literacy foundation.

The Giants pulled off an improbable 17–14 victory and many thought Tuck deserved the MVP award after he harassed Brady for the duration of the game and recorded two sacks, a forced fumble and five tackles. However, after being responsible for so much of the Giants' success in 2007, Tuck's defensive line was depleted the following year — Strahan retired

and Umenyiora was lost for the season because of knee surgery. Tuck took it upon himself to be the new leader and ended up with a career-high 12 sacks and 67 tackles.

Tuck played every game over the next two seasons, but missed four games in 2011, battling injuries to his neck, shoulder, groin and toe. His effectiveness was limited, but he shone when it mattered most, recording 5.5 sacks in the Giants' last six wins of the season, all of which were crucial toward making the playoffs.

"We know he's hurting," defensive tackle Chris Canty said at the time. "But when you're in your stance at the line and turn your head and see that he's putting it out there for the team — and then making big plays — that gets everybody fired up."

After squeaking into the playoffs on the final day of the regular season, the Giants played like it was the 2007 season all over again. They crushed the Atlanta Falcons in their hometown before upsetting the Green Bay Packers and San Francisco 49ers to make it to the Super Bowl. Tuck saved his best for last, with 1.5 sacks in the NFC championship game against the 49ers and two more in Super Bowl XLVI against Brady and the Patriots.

Tuck was a thorn in Brady's Ugg boots once again. On the Patriots' first possession, Tuck chased Brady into his own end zone, forcing him to throw away the ball for an illegal grounding penalty, which resulted in a safety that gave the Giants the first two points of the game. Tuck finished strong, and his two sacks came on the Patriots' final three possessions that helped seal the Giants' 21–17 victory.

Tuck walked off the field in Indianapolis with his second Super Bowl win and no reason to be debriefed. He had earned his ring and could be secure in the knowledge that he was (and is) ranked among the best in the game and is well on his way to becoming known as a New York Giant legend.

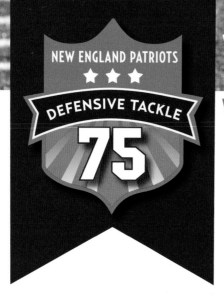

NEW ENGLAND PATRIOTS
★ ★ ★
DEFENSIVE TACKLE
75

VINCE WILFORK

At 6-foot-2 and approximately 325 pounds, Vince Wilfork is a mountain of a man, but he is deceptively quick when he's on the hunt. Thanks to his considerable weight, Wilfork excelled behind the shot put at Santaluces High School in Lantana, Florida, and set a state record that still stands. He was, however, also light enough on his feet to be a running back and to return punts on top of his defensive-line duties for his high school football team.

Wilfork continued to multitask at the University of Miami, where he was on the track and field team as a shot-putter and discus thrower. He was equally adept, of course, at chucking offensive linemen around — and in his freshman year he had 148 tackles, including 73 solo, with 14 sacks for losses of 60 yards and 37.5 stops for losses of 110 yards. He also had 42 quarterback pressures, 5 forced fumbles and 3 fumble recoveries.

In Wilfork's junior year, he was named the best defensive tackle in the country by the NFL Draft Report, so he skipped his senior season and declared himself eligible for the 2004 draft. He was selected by the New England Patriots as the 21st overall pick, and they immediately suggested that he slim down.

"I played at 345 pounds in college, every snap, in the heat," says Wilfork. "Up here they want me at 325. They tell me if you're 20 pounds lighter, you're going to do this or that better. That's a bunch of baloney. I don't buy it. As a player I don't feel stronger or faster at 325.

- Four-time Pro Bowl selection (2007, 2009–2011)
- Three-time All-Pro (2007, 2010, 2011)
- Super Bowl champion (XXXIX)
- All-American Dream Team and unanimous All-Big East with the University of Miami (2003)

I've had a hard time coping with that. But that's just me."

Whatever his weight, Wilfork's work has paid off. In his first season with the Patriots, they won the Super Bowl, and in his 122 regular-season games, the team sits at a .779 winning percentage. Wilfork has also been defensive co-captain four times, played in the Pro Bowl four times, helped the Patriots to a top-10 defense four times and been part of the 2007 Patriots team that went undefeated in the regular season and set an NFL record by outscoring their opponents by 315 points.

IN THE HUDDLE
Underneath Wilfork's jersey, he wears a small locket with his parents' high school prom picture in it; he lost his mother and father within five months of each other when he was playing at the University of Miami.

In the 2011 season, New England's defense was not a top-10 unit and was actually viewed as a liability, but Wilfork dragged his teammates to Super Bowl XLVI with 15 tackles and 3.5 sacks in the 4 games leading up to the championship.

Wilfork was particularly dominant in the AFC Championship. The Baltimore Ravens' elite running back Ray Rice was held to 67 yards on 21 carries in the game, including 11 runs of 2 yards or less, and that last stat is thanks to Wilfork filling the gap and overpowering Rice's blockers. Wilfork was also relentless in harassing and hurrying Ravens quarterback Joe Flacco throughout the entire game. The Patriots needed Wilfork's skills on a day that the Ravens' vaunted defense was holding Tom Brady and his offensive weapons in check, and in the end, it was an ugly 23–20 New England victory in a game that was won in the trenches with Wilfork leading the charge.

With Wilfork, however, it always comes back to weight.

"Well, if you had asked me to guess, I wouldn't have said anything close to 325," says Terrance Knighton, a 336-pound tackle with the Jacksonville Jaguars. "But if that's what Wilfork says, he's a good player and he's a lot older than me, and he's been playing this position longer than me. So 325 it is."

Wilfork is well aware of the dangers associated with a high weight — he and his wife Bianca host an annual fundraiser for the Diabetes Research Institute and he is consistently monitored for the disease, which claimed his father at age 48. Wilfork also has three children, and he says he wants to live to be a grandparent, which his own parents didn't get to do. "The last thing I want is to get sick with something I could have changed. When I stop playing, man, I'll be so small you won't even recognize me."

For now, though, his incredible bulk isn't just taking up space, it's changing the game.

"It's misleading because you see him in short bursts," says football analyst Chris Schultz, a former NFL player. "But what you don't understand is how fast the bursts happen and how violent the bursts are. I'm not sure people understand how hard guys like Wilfork work. He's a phenomenal athlete in his role."

LINEBACKERS

★ ★ ★

LANCE BRIGGS — Chicago Bears

LONDON FLETCHER — Washington Redskins

TAMBA HALI — Kansas City Chiefs

JAMES HARRISON — Pittsburgh Steelers

RAY LEWIS — Baltimore Ravens

CLAY MATTHEWS — Green Bay Packers

VON MILLER — Denver Brocos

TERRELL SUGGS — Baltimore Ravens

BRIAN URLACHER — Chicago Bears

DEMARCUS WARE — Dallas Cowboys

MARIO WILLIAMS — Buffalo Bills

PATRICK WILLIS — San Francisco 49ers

★ ★ ★

CHICAGO BEARS
★ ★ ★
LINEBACKER
55

LANCE BRIGGS

Chicago Bears linebacker Lance Briggs has been a comic book aficionado since he got his first *X-Men* comic when he was seven years old, and the nice part about growing up to be an NFL star is that it provides the money and freedom to explore passions. In Briggs' case, he created and co-wrote a comic book about a character named Seraph who "combines faith and action" and goes from being a sinner to a saint; Briggs now sells his work on lancescomicworld.com, the comic-book social network he started.

Briggs, however, wasn't exactly a nerd while growing up in Sacramento, California. Yes, he likely obsessed over comics, but he was also a track star and an exceptional football player. At Elk Grove High School, he was named Sacramento Player of the Year by the *Sacramento Bee* newspaper for his work as linebacker, running back, safety, kicker and punt returner, and later, at the University of Arizona, Briggs was a three-time All-Pac 10 selection after switching from fullback to linebacker after his freshman year. In his sophomore season he was first on the team with 113 tackles, and followed that by leading the Wildcats the next two years.

After a stellar college career, Briggs was expecting to be a high draft pick in 2003, but his pro-day workout didn't go as planned. Dehydrated after trying to lose some weight, Briggs performed poorly and his stock plummeted — all the way to the third round, where the Bears finally selected him.

"Oh, man, it was terrible, one of the longest days of my life," says Briggs of draft day. "I was the 13th linebacker drafted, and I can name all 12 of the guys who went ahead of me. … So yeah, I use it as motivation."

That motivation has created a 6-foot-1, 244-pound superhero with super-speed, agility and strength that allows Briggs to cover large swaths of the field and punish opponents who dare to invade the Bears' turf. Briggs has more than 100 tackles in seven of his nine NFL seasons, and during almost every one of those seasons has alternated with fellow All-Pro and face-of-the-franchise Brian Urlacher as the team leader in tackles. In 2005 and 2006, they became the first Bears linebackers since Mike Singletary and Wilber Marshall in 1987 and 1988 to be named to consecutive Pro Bowls together.

IN THE HUDDLE
After his Pro Bowl selection in 2010, Briggs became the fourth linebacker in Bears history to be selected to the game six times, joining Hall of Famers Dick Butkus, Bill George and Mike Singletary. In 2011 he was named to his seventh Pro Bowl.

While Briggs is often overshadowed by Urlacher, they are good friends who are competitive both on and off the field, as they are known to battle each other in ping-pong

CAREER HIGHLIGHTS
- Seven-time Pro Bowl selection (2005–2011)
- Three-time All-Pro (2005, 2006, 2009)
- Most tackles for negative yards of any linebacker in the league, and is second overall
- Became the first linebacker in NFL history to return an interception for a touchdown in each of his first three seasons
- Fourth Bear to have over 1,000 tackles since the stat started being recorded in 1971

and bowling matches and rib each other when one has more tackles than the other.

Briggs, however, is managing to carve his own niche among the legendary linebackers (collectively known as the Monsters of the Midway) who have defined the Bears. Briggs ranks in the top four in team history for career tackles, interceptions for touchdowns and Pro Bowl selections, which are feats that put him in impressive company for a franchise that is steeped in tradition at the linebacker position.

The passion that drives Briggs to these heights burns off the field as well, and it is a stimulant that has caused a few problems for management. Briggs crashed his Lamborghini on a Chicago highway and left the scene, which led to a heavy fine and community service, and on more than one occasion he has proclaimed he had played his last down with the Bears. It also doesn't help that his agent is

Drew Rosenhaus, a man who is known for his bellicosity.

Prior to the 2011 season, when the Bears said they were honoring the contract Briggs signed through 2013 instead of restructuring it, he requested a trade. But, once the season began, Briggs put his distractions aside and had over 100 tackles yet again. As Briggs said when contemplating a holdout in 2007: "I can earn more respect, and money, by getting out on the field and playing, and proving that I am who I believe I am."

Briggs and the Chicago defense were strong in 2011 and the team was poised for a playoff run, but they lost quarterback Jay Cutler and main offensive threat Matt Forte midway through the season. The team went into a tailspin and missed the playoffs.

Moving forward, if Briggs can act as Seraph has and use his powers for good, he, too, might become a hero by leading the Bears back to the promised land.

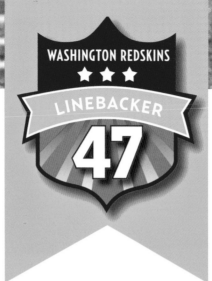

LONDON FLETCHER

In November 2007, intruders broke into the home of Washington Redskins safety and fan favorite Sean Taylor and shot him as he slept. He died a day later, and the Redskins were left with a massive void, both on the field and in the locker room. In the team's first game after Taylor's death, the defense lined up with 10 men on the field (one less than the customary 11) to honor his memory.

One of those 10 was inside linebacker London Fletcher, a former Buffalo Bill who the Redskins had signed in the off-season to be a team leader. It was time for him to step up and guide the Redskins through the aftermath of the tragedy while still being the backbone of the defense. Four seasons later, Fletcher has done all of what the team asked of him — and more.

When he finished college, not one scout could have predicted Fletcher would be in the position he is today. Unlike the majority of pro football players, he didn't play for a traditional college powerhouse. Instead, he played Division III ball for the John Carroll University Blue Streaks.

Because of the lack of exposure, Fletcher went undrafted and signed as a free agent with the St. Louis Rams, making the team out of training camp. He ended up playing in all 16 games in 1998 and winning the Rams' Rookie of the Year Award.

In the 1999 season, Fletcher led

CAREER HIGHLIGHTS

- Super Bowl Champion with the St Louis Rams (1999)

- Walter Payton NFL Man of the Year nominee (2005, 2006, 2008, 2009)

- Two-time Pro Bowl selection (2010, 2011)

- Washington Redskins Inaugural Community Service Award (2011)

- Call to Courage Award (2011)

- Second Team All-Pro (2011)

- Combined tackles leader (2011)

the team in tackles, and the Rams went on to beat the Tennessee Titans 23–16 in Super Bowl XXXIV. The following year, Fletcher established the franchise record for tackles in a season (193), and in 2001, the Rams nearly won their second Super Bowl in three years, losing 20–17 to the New England Patriots on a last-second field goal.

The Bills wisely chose to sign Fletcher as an unrestricted free agent in 2002, and he stayed in Buffalo for five seasons, averaging 145 tackles a year. His best season there was his last, when he had a team-high 157 tackles, including nine for loss, a career-best 14 deflections and four interceptions. He also collected his first career touchdown 12 seconds into the regular-season opener against the Patriots. Following the 2006 season, Fletcher became an unrestricted free agent and the Redskins signed him to a five-year, $25 million contract.

Fletcher is considered undersized at 5-foot-10 and 245 pounds, but

he uses his instincts and speed to remain — 14 years after breaking into the Rams lineup — one of the NFL's best and most ferocious hitters. In all those years, Fletcher has never missed a game and the wear and tear of the sport hasn't slowed him down; in 2011, he led the league in tackles (166) for a Washington team that has struggled mightily.

IN THE HUDDLE
Fletcher has been compared to perennial Emmy Award runner-up Susan Lucci because he was a Pro Bowl alternate nine seasons in a row before making the team in 2010 and 2011.

The mental aspect of football can be just as taxing as the physical, but after years of dysfunction and falling short of the playoffs, Fletcher still believes in the Redskins and chooses to be optimistic about the team's future. "I love playing here in D.C., and the organization has been

great to me. I still feel like I'd like to be a part of bringing back that winning tradition to the Redskins. I know I keep saying it, but that's just how I feel."

Fletcher's teammates, whom he personally organized and led through workouts during the lockout in 2011, believe in his words. "He's the captain of our ship," says reserve cornerback Byron Westbrook. "He's vocal. He has a lot of passion. He's always positive and upbeat. Guys want to follow a leader like that."

Promising young linebacker Brian Orakpo agrees. "When he [Fletcher] sees guys in the huddle with their heads down, he's always bringing them back up. That's what I really respect about him. He's always the same."

Fletcher's contract ran out at the end of the 2011 season, and in April the Redskins wisely resigned him. As the elder statesman, the 37 year old can now focus on leading the Red Skins back to glory.

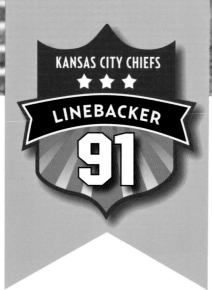

KANSAS CITY CHIEFS
★ ★ ★
LINEBACKER
91

TAMBA HALI

Everyone takes a different path to the NFL, but rarely does it include living in the African jungle, fleeing a civil war and leaving your mother behind at the age of 10. For the Kansas City Chiefs' Tamba Hali, this was his reality, and it's what motivated him to succeed.

Born in Suacoco, Liberia, and raised in the capital city of Monrovia, Hali was six when war broke out in his homeland, forcing his family to periodically live in the wilderness to hide from the indiscriminate killing that was happening around them. In 1994, Hali escaped across the eastern border and into the Ivory Coast with his sister and two half-brothers, and they eventually made their way to Teaneck, New Jersey, to live with their father, Henry, who had left Liberia when Hali was two years old. His mother, Rachel, had never officially married Henry, so she wasn't eligible to be sponsored to come to the U.S. It was 12 years before Hali saw her again.

English is the native language of Liberia, but Hali hadn't received a formal education and had to learn to read and write. He was teased about his accent, but discovered a home and a voice on the football field.

CAREER HIGHLIGHTS

- 2005 All-American
- 2005 Big Ten Defensive Lineman of the Year
- 2006 Senior Bowl Defensive MVP
- 2006 NFL All-Rookie
- *USA Today* All-Joe Team (2009)
- Two-time Pro Bowl selection (2010, 2011)
- AFC sack leader with 14.5 (2010)

"I found myself enjoying myself when I was playing the game," says Hali. "Just being out there, having fun with my teammates … But I didn't even know about college scholarships. I was just playing to play. When I first got offered [a scholarship] by Boston College, I went to my coach and said, 'What am I supposed to say to the guy?'"

Hali ended up accepting a scholarship to Penn State University, a.k.a. Linebacker U, where he was a consensus All-American and the unanimous selection as the Big Ten Defensive Lineman of the Year in 2005. That season, he helped the Nittany Lions to an 11–1 record and a 26–23 victory over Florida State University in the Orange Bowl. If his achievements weren't enough to impress scouts, his speech at the 2006 draft combine was.

"I was just overwhelmed, not only with his story, but the way he told it," says Ernie Accorsi, general manager of the New York Giants the year Hali was drafted. "He's such a thoughtful, intellectual, moving person. You could hear a pin drop in our interview room when he was done telling his story."

Hali didn't end up with the Giants, however, and the Chiefs took him with the 20th pick in the draft. That would have been the highlight of most football players' draft year, if not their lives, but Hali had more important things happening. In July, he left rookie camp for a day to be sworn in as an American citizen, and in September he saw his mother for the first time since he was 10 years old.

IN THE HUDDLE

Hali is 6-foot-3 and 275 pounds, but he's still known as "Little Tamba" at the family dinner table because his older half-brother is also named Tamba; Chiefs fans call him "TambaHawk."

"I'm playing for her," Hali said before she was able to come to the U.S. "Every time I get to the ball, every time I make my name more known, I feel like I'm closer to her."

As a rookie, Hali led the Chiefs with eight sacks, 3.5 more than first-overall-pick outside linebacker Mario Williams of the Houston Texans. After replacing all-world pass rusher and personality Jared Allen on the right side in 2008 and then moving to outside linebacker in

2009, Hali had a breakout year in 2010, recording 14.5 sacks to lead the AFC. The Chiefs rewarded him after the season with a five-year, $60 million contract, making him the second-highest-paid outside linebacker in the league behind the Dallas Cowboys' DeMarcus Ware.

It's money well spent for the Chiefs, according to Matt Williamson of Scouts, Inc. Hali isn't just the best player on the Chiefs; he's the best player in the AFC West, and his work ethic has kept him from getting lazy after signing a fat new contract. In 2011, Hali had 12 sacks, despite not having another pass rushing threat on the opposite side to attract attention from the opponent's best blockers. He was also instrumental in handing the Green Bay Packers their only loss of the season as he recorded three sacks on the day.

"I believe in working," says Hali. "Me impressing myself is not really important. It's about working. Since I've been here, you really just don't say much, and you work, so success is going to come."

Indeed, Hali doesn't have to say much — his story's been told and now he's letting his play do the talking.

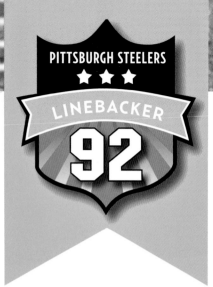

JAMES HARRISON

A player doesn't last long in the NFL trenches if they don't play with equal parts edge and anger, and most linemen know when to unleash the fury and when to keep it within the boundaries of the game, but most linemen are not James Harrison.

Growing up in Akron, Ohio, Harrison was the youngest of 14 kids, and his mother, Mildred, taught young James about "standing up for what he believes in and saying what he wants."

At Coventry High School, Harrison was a running back, a linebacker and a handful. He was suspended for threatening an assistant coach and making lewd gestures at opposing fans, and he was arrested for shooting a BB gun in the locker room.

According to Mo Tipton, Harrison's head coach at Coventry, "He was the most physically tough player I've ever been around, but he had some anger problems off the field."

Harrison's behavioral issues scared off the major college programs and cost him a scholarship to Kent State University, but not his spot on the team — his parents borrowed money to send him to school, and after improving on his grades, he led the Kent State football team to its first winning season in 14 years.

Harrison was a first-team All-Mid-American Conference player, and while he led the conference in sacks, he went undrafted. The Pittsburgh Steelers signed him as a free agent in 2002 and then released, re-signed and released him again in 2003. Harrison shuttled between the practice squad and the active roster several times before leaving briefly to join the Baltimore Ravens, who sent him to Germany to play with the Rhein Fire of NFL Europe. He rejoined the Steelers in 2004.

IN THE HUDDLE
Harrison is the only undrafted player to be named Defensive Player of the Year.

An injury to a regular roster player is what gave Harrison his first real chance to play meaningful football for the Steelers, but he still had to wait three years, until 2007, to start a game. When he finally did take the field on the first opposition drive, it was against the Ravens, and he took out his frustrations, collecting 3.5 sacks, 10 tackles, 3 forced fumbles, 1 recovery and 1 interception.

Harrison led the Steelers in sacks and finished second in tackles in 2007, and in 2008, he exploded with 16 sacks, 101 tackles and 7 forced fumbles to be named

CAREER HIGHLIGHTS

- Five-time Pro Bowl selection (2007–2011)
- Four-time All-Pro (2007–2010)
- Two-time Super Bowl champion (XL, XLIII)
- Defensive Player of the Year (2008)
- Holds the Steelers' single-season sack record (16)
- Returned an interception 100 yards for a touchdown in Super Bowl XLIII, which is the longest play in Super Bowl history

Defensive Player of the Year.

As big a surprise as Harrison's breakout year was, what he did later that year in Super Bowl XLIII was a shock. The Arizona Cardinals were on the Steelers' goal line looking to take a lead into the locker room as the first half wound down. Quarterback Kurt Warner dropped back to pass and Harrison read it perfectly, intercepting the ball and rumbling 100 yards for a touchdown. It was the longest-scoring play in Super Bowl history and it gave the Steelers a 17–7 lead in a game they won 27–23.

There is no doubt that Harrison takes the game seriously, and it is well known that he is obsessed with fine-tuning his body with a combination of old-school workouts in the Arizona desert, acupuncture and oxygen therapy in a hyperbaric chamber. And, yes, he's relatively undersized at 6-feet-tall and 242 pounds, but the chip on his shoulder is massive, and this was no more evident than during the 2010 season. This was the year injury concerns in the NFL literally came to a head. After a series of devastating concussions, the NFL cracked down on violent hits and Harrison took the brunt of the wrath, incurring a

record $120,000 in fines, including $75,000 for a knockout blow to Cleveland Browns receiver Mohamed Massaquoi.

"There's a river of people that want to cheat me," Harrison's been known to say, and he was further able to air his grievances in a *Men's Journal* article in 2011. Beside a picture of Harrison posing shirtless while holding two of his own firearms, he was quoted taking a shot at the most powerful man in football — commissioner Roger Goodell.

"My rep is James Harrison, mean son of a bitch who loves

hitting the hell out of people," Harrison said in the interview. "But up until last year, there was no word of me being dirty — till Roger Goodell, who's a crook and a puppet, said I was the dirtiest player in the league … I hate him and will never respect him."

Strong words from an angry man, who has used slights against him, whether they're perceived or real, to become one of the most feared and ferocious men in the NFL and the history of the Steelers. Opponents and league administration, you've been warned.

BALTIMORE RAVENS
★ ★ ★
LINEBACKER
52

RAY LEWIS

The story of Ray Lewis is Shakespearean in its familial relationships, tragedy, murder and redemption, and the man himself is a character full of sound and fury.

Growing up in Lakeland, Florida, Lewis eventually took the last name of a family friend because his father, Elbert Ray Jackson — a man with whom he has next to no relationship — would disappear for long stretches of time.

In high school, Lewis also helped raise his five younger siblings while systematically erasing Jackson's name from the Kathleen High School

wrestling record books and making his own mark on the football field.

Later, at the University of Miami, Lewis had 17 tackles in his first start and confidently declared he would be the best Hurricane ever. He led the team in tackles for 22 straight games, had the second-highest single-season total in team history and finished with 388 tackles before declaring himself eligible for the draft after his junior year.

Lewis' time at Miami was, however, touched by grief — fellow linebacker and best friend Marlin

Barnes was beaten to death in the apartment the pair shared.

Barnes' funeral was held the day the Baltimore Ravens drafted Lewis 26th overall in 1996. Lewis' anger at the world fueled a successful start to his career on the field but created a messy life off of it.

Named Defensive Player of the Year in 2000 after the Ravens established a 16-game single-season record for fewest points allowed (165) and fewest rushing yards allowed (970), Lewis also posted four shutouts and finished first in six defensive categories.

CAREER HIGHLIGHTS

- Thirteen-time Pro Bowl selection (1997–2001, 2003, 2004, 2006–2011)

- Ten-time All-Pro (1997–2001, 2003, 2004, 2008–2010)

- Two-time Defensive Player of the Year (2000, 2003)

- Super Bowl XXXV champion

- Super Bowl XXXV MVP

- NFL All-Decade Team for the 2000s

This was also the year he spent 15 days in prison facing double murder charges when two men were stabbed outside an Atlanta nightclub on the night of the Super Bowl. The charges were eventually dropped because of a lack of evidence, but general suspicion remained and Lewis was a pariah everywhere but Baltimore.

Lewis persevered and less than one year later, the Ravens held the New York Giants without an offensive touchdown to win 34–7 in Super Bowl XXXV. Lewis made 5 tackles and blocked 4 passes to be named Super Bowl MVP, and was only the second linebacker to win the award as well as the first to receive it in 30 years. Meanwhile, outside the stadium, the aunt of one of the Atlanta murder victims was demanding justice. She later recanted her position and professed her belief in Lewis' innocence, he took it as a sign to change his ways. The mayhem on the field didn't relent, but Lewis' actions away from the game showed signs of growth and maturity. He became a better father to his children and he started investing in his community through the Ray Lewis Family Foundation.

IN THE HUDDLE
Lewis is the NFL's active leader in tackles and was the quickest player in NFL history to join the 20 sacks/20 interception club, was the quickest to reach 30/30, and in 2011 became the only member of the 40/30 club.

Lewis is a beloved figure in Baltimore thanks to his annual gifts of school supplies and Thanksgiving turkeys for those less fortunate, and it doesn't hurt that the Ravens have ranked in the top 10 in fewest yards allowed in 9 straight seasons and have held opponents under 4.0 yards per rush for each of the 16 years Lewis has been on the team, which is the longest streak in NFL history.

Arguably the greatest linebacker in the history of the NFL, Lewis has a "pureness of his heart," according to former Ravens linebackers coach Mike Singletary, who is one of Lewis' closest allies and mentors.

Tatyana McCall, who has three sons with Lewis, agrees: "Ray has a huge heart and will help anybody in need if he's able. I would be remiss if I didn't say I was proud to be the mother of his kids. It's not always easy, but I am very proud."

In 2011, Lewis had 95 tackles to lead the team for the 14th time, despite missing 4 games with a foot injury. He also has 13 seasons with at least 130 tackles and has 13 Pro Bowl appearances. Further, he's first in the Ravens' history books with 2,586 tackles — second on the list is Kelly Gregg with 721.

But the only thing more relentless than Lewis is time; the game always ends and eventually his career will too, and when it does, Lewis, who puts consecrated oil on his teammates' foreheads, plans on starting a worldwide ministry. With a life story such as it is, Lewis should have people lining up to hear his tales of salvation — all delivered with his signature swagger and touch of menace.

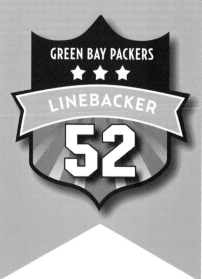

CLAY MATTHEWS

Clay Matthews III is the scion of football royalty, but that doesn't mean the game came easily or that his path to the NFL was assured. Matthews descends from Clay Sr., who played defensive end for four seasons with the San Francisco 49ers, and from Clay Jr., who was a linebacker for 19 seasons with the Cleveland Browns and the Atlanta Falcons. Growing up, however, there was little indication that

Matthews was going to be the one to make his family only the second in NFL history to place three generations of players.

As a junior at Agoura Hills High School in Agoura, California, Matthews weighed 166 pounds soaking wet, which is the main reason his father, the team's defensive coordinator, kept him off the field. Luckily, Matthews had a growth spurt in his senior season and became a starter for the first time, but there was no college recruitment to speak of.

Matthews enrolled at the University of Southern California anyway and tried out for the Trojans as a walk-on. After sitting out a year, he earned a scholarship in his sophomore season, but it was a loaded USC team and, as in high school, he only became a starter in his senior year.

But, even as a late bloomer, Matthews still played in four straight Rose Bowls, was named a USC Special Teams Player of the Year three times and in the Senior Bowl had a game-high six tackles, including a sack, two fumble recoveries and a forced fumble.

It was an impressive showing that caused the Green Bay Packers' general manager Ted Thompson to break with his own tradition and trade up into the

first round to get Matthews, who was picked 26th overall in 2009.

A hamstring injury held Matthews back in training camp and the preseason, but he deviated from his own history of slow starts and burst onto the NFL scene with a first year to remember. Playing in all 16 games, Matthews set a franchise rookie record with 10 sacks and also became the first rookie to lead the team in sacks since 1986. Further, he was the first Green Bay rookie to be named to the Pro Bowl since 1978.

IN THE HUDDLE

Matthews is the first Packer with double-digit sack totals in each of his first two seasons. He is also the first Packer with a sack in each of his first three playoff games. His 17 sacks in his first 20 NFL games is a league record.

Avoiding the sophomore slump and proving he was no fluke, Matthews upped his numbers in his second season with 13.5 sacks, 85 tackles and 40 quarterback hits. He also had his first career interception, which he ran back for his first touchdown during a prime-time game against the Dallas Cowboys.

This memorable season was capped by an unlikely Super Bowl run, with the Packers victorious in their final game of the season (a

must-win to get into the playoffs), and then winning three road games to reach the Super Bowl. In these three games, Matthews had 3.5 sacks (a franchise record for one postseason), and in Super Bowl XLV against the Pittsburgh Steelers he made — arguably — the most important defensive play of the season.

At the start of the fourth quarter, the Packers were clinging to a 21–17 lead with the Steelers driving. Anticipating a run, Matthews told defensive end Ryan Pickett to push the runner outside, where Matthews met Pittsburgh's Rashard Mendenhall with a high hit that knocked the ball loose. Green Bay recovered the fumble and scored a touchdown on the ensuing drive, which ultimately made the difference in their 31–25 victory.

Matthews did it all on a broken leg. "I don't make a big deal of it," he said. "[It happened] sometime in the middle of the season. You can't do anything about it. I was just taking practices off and showing up on game day and giving it my all."

Although Matthews' leg was healed in 2011, his numbers were down; constant double– and triple-teaming kept him from racking up sacks and a weakened defense allowed teams to focus on him, but he still had career highs in pass deflections and interceptions and the Packers finished 15–1 in the regular season.

This time the Packers were favorites heading into the playoffs, but they lost at home to the New York Giants, who went on to win the championship the Packers were defending.

CAREER HIGHLIGHTS
- Three-time Pro Bowl selection (2009–11)
- All-Pro (2010)
- Super Bowl XLV champion
- NFC Defensive Player of the Year (2010)
- Dick Butkus Award (2010)

If Matthews continues at the torrid pace he has set, he might one day join his uncle, Bruce Matthews, in the Hall of Fame. Besides, with his younger brother Casey on the Philadelphia Eagles' roster and his cousin Kevin playing for the Tennessee Titans, it's clear that the Matthews family is no ordinary clan.

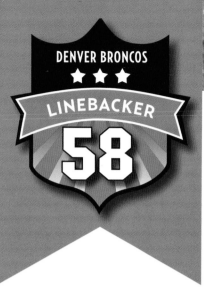

DENVER BRONCOS
★ ★ ★

LINEBACKER

58

VON MILLER

CAREER HIGHLIGHTS

- NFL Defensive Rookie of the Year (2011)
- All-Pro (2011)
- Pro Bowl (2011)
- Butkus Award winner as the nation's top linebacker (2010)
- First-team All-American (2009, 2010)
- First-team All-Big 12 (2009, 2010)

Second-year quarterback Tim Tebow may have hogged the headlines in Denver in 2011, but it was first-year linebacker Von Miller who took home the hardware and who is on track to become a Broncos legend.

Miller grew up in DeSoto, Texas, where he played high school football and became one of the best defensive-end prospects in Texas. He chose to continue his football career with Texas A&M University, which was where, after getting by rather easily, his life and football path became much more serious. Following Miller's freshman year, former Green Bay Packers coach Mike Sherman took over the program and Miller could suddenly no longer get by on raw talent alone. This was evident when, prior to his sophomore year, Sherman suspended Miller indefinitely … or until he started taking practices and schoolwork seriously. He considered transferring colleges, but his father reminded him he had made a commitment to the university and to the team. Thus, with a new sense of purpose, Miller put his nose to the grindstone.

After Sherman welcomed Miller back to the team, his new work ethic paid almost immediate dividends, and in his junior year was installed as a hybrid defensive end/ outside linebacker, a position that

was called "Joker." That season, Miller led the country in sacks with 17 and was fifth with 21.5 tackles for losses.

In his senior year, the 6-foot-3, 245-pound Miller battled an ankle injury and his numbers went down slightly, but his 10.5 sacks and 17.5 tackles behind the line of scrimmage still earned him the Butkus Award as the country's best linebacker. He was also named as a first-team All-Big 12 and an All-American for the second year in a row.

IN THE HUDDLE

Miller wears the number 58 to honor his favorite player, the late Derrick Thomas, whom he studied extensively while he was in school and who sacked his boss, Broncos executive vice president John Elway, more than any other player during his Hall of Fame career.

After dominating at the Senior Bowl, Miller was approached by veteran running back LaDainian Tomlinson. He asked Miller to take part in the lawsuit against the NFL that the players were filing as part of the lockout negotiations. As a high-profile pick in the upcoming draft, Miller said yes and essentially ended up representing all the young players who were entering the league. "The PA [Players'

Association] could've picked any rookie coming out this year," Miller said at the time. "It's a blessing that fell into my lap."

Thus, before his NFL career even started, Miller was already making a name for himself among the likes of Peyton Manning, Tom Brady and Drew Brees. Then, after being drafted second overall by the Broncos, Miller stocked up his trophy shelf in his rookie year — he was named to the All-Pro and Pro Bowl teams and won Defensive Rookie of the Year.

Additionally, Miller's first NFL play was one of his most memorable sacks — he forced a fumble that helped seal a win the Broncos needed during a six-game winning streak. Lined up against the New York Jets' Wayne Hunter, who outweighed Miller by 75 pounds,

he simply ran straight into Hunter, knocked him over and tackled quarterback Mark Sanchez for an eight-yard loss.

With 11.5 sacks (including 6 in his first 6 games), 64 tackles and 3 forced fumbles, Miller was the most disruptive and electrifying force on the Denver defense. During the last four games of the season, he even played with a cast on his surgically repaired thumb, which exemplified the kind of grit and determination the entire defense showed in dragging the Broncos into the playoffs and upsetting the Pittsburgh Steelers in the first round.

"I'm going to attack and give relentless effort, fanatical effort," said Miller. "That's my formula, and I'm sticking to it. I try to get off the ball as fast as possible and react to whatever the offense is trying

to do to me. I don't really have any premeditated moves."

Miller, however, still played with an edge and a youthful exuberance, and he was fined three times during his rookie year. The third fine was handed down after he shoved the New England Patriots' offensive lineman Dan Connolly, and Miller's impulsive action sparked a melee following Brady's punt in the Broncos' blowout playoff loss to the Patriots.

In the offseason, the Broncos traded Tebow and signed premier quarterback Peyton Manning. The lights in Denver will no doubt be on Manning, no matter what the Broncos do in 2012, but it will be Miller who will again lead the defensive charge, and be just as important as Manning to the fate of the Denver Broncos.

BALTIMORE RAVENS
★ ★ ★
LINEBACKER
55

TERRELL SUGGS

B altimore Ravens linebacker Terrell "Sizzle" Suggs isn't your average jock — as part of Team Sizzle, his production company, he co-wrote and produced *When Beautiful People Do Ugly Things*, a short film that was shot in Baltimore and shown at the Cannes Film Festival in 2011. According to the Team Sizzle website, "Terrell Suggs has always had three very definitive dreams. To play professional football, to be a wonderful father and to be a filmmaker."

Suggs definitely has the football part covered, but he is not your average player. Born in Minneapolis, Suggs played football with future Major League Baseball MVP Joe Mauer before moving to Arizona and attending three different high schools. The man who now (in the NFL) stops the run then led the state with 2,274 yards rushing, including one game with 367 yards and 5 touchdowns.

After graduating from Chandler, Arizona's Hamilton High School as an All-American and Arizona Player of the Year, Suggs went to Arizona State University to play as a linebacker instead of a running back. While there, he set school records for career sacks (44) and tackles for a loss (65.5), and in his third and final year he obliterated the NCAA record for single-season sacks (24), making him the easy choice as team MVP, unanimous All-American, winner of the Bronko Nagurski Trophy as the country's top defensive player and recipient of the Rotary Lombardi Award for college lineman of the year.

Suggs was picked 10th overall by the Ravens in the 2003 draft, and he tied an NFL record with a sack in each of his first four games in the NFL. Suggs finished the season with a Ravens rookie-record 12 sacks to earn the Defensive Rookie of the Year award.

IN THE HUDDLE

Suggs is the Baltimore Ravens' all-time leader in regular-season sacks and sack yardage (82.5 for 610 yards), and in postseason yardage (10 for 69 yards).

In 2005, the Ravens' defensive guru and current New York Jets head coach Rex Ryan had Suggs alternate between outside linebacker and defensive end, which was a move that dropped his sack total but also upped his tackles and made him the multipurpose defensive threat who went on to appear in eight Pro Bowls, make two All-Pro teams and become the Ravens' all-time leader in forced fumbles, as well as regular-season and postseason sacks.

Before facing Ryan as coach of the New York Jets early in the 2011 season, Suggs said: "I love playing against Rex, because I think he gets to see his finest work up close. If he's Michelangelo, I was his Sistine Chapel. He gets to see what he created. He gets to coach against the very beast, the monster he helped create."

The 2011 season was a masterpiece for Suggs. He was the best player on a defensive unit that was ranked third in the league in total yardage allowed, second in stopping the run and first in red-zone defense. Suggs led the AFC with a career-high 14 sacks, his 7 forced fumbles set a single-season Ravens record and were the most

in the NFL that season. To top it all off he also tied career highs with 6 pass deflections and 2 interceptions.

For Suggs, it all added up to an NFL Defensive Player of the Year award, but, ultimately, the season was a failure for his team. In the AFC Championship, the Ravens' defense managed to frustrate Tom Brady and the New England Patriots, but a botched field goal cost Baltimore a chance for overtime and a trip to the Super Bowl.

Suggs will likely have other opportunities; the Ravens have twice kept him on the team by designating him as their franchise player, and in 2008, he signed a six-year, $62.5 million contract that included $38 million in guaranteed money, which made him the highest-paid linebacker in the league.

For Suggs, the money meant the freedom to set up a mini-theatre in his locker and the ability to produce five films and take one to Cannes in France. Suggs, however, hasn't gone Hollywood. "At the end of the day, I'm always going to be Terrell," he says. "I've got to go home to my kids. That's humbling. There's no football player or filmmaker there. It's just daddy."

Sounding like the doting father he is, Suggs is nonetheless estranged from the mother of his children and has been sued by her. He endured further public controversy in 2011 when he openly insulted ESPN personality Skip Bayless and derisively questioned whether God was really cheering for Tim Tebow.

Suggs will have plenty of time to make incendiary comments this season, as he tore his Achilles tendon in the off-season and is expected to be out all year.

Suggs insists he'll prove people wrong and play in 2012; he does tend to realize his goals, so don't count the "Sizzle" out just yet.

CAREER HIGHLIGHTS

- Five-time Pro Bowl selection (2004, 2006, 2008, 2010, 2011)

- Two-time All-Pro (2008, 2011)

- 2011 Defensive Player of the Year

- 2003 Defensive Rookie of the Year

- Owns the Ravens' single-season and all-time forced fumbles records (7 in 2011, 29 all-time)

- Consensus All-American (2002)

- 2002 winner of the Bronko Nagurski Trophy and the Rotary Lombardi Award

CHICAGO BEARS
★ ★ ★
LINEBACKER
54

BRIAN URLACHER

B rian Urlacher learned two very important lessons as a teenager: one, the value of hard work, came from his mother, Lavoyda, who worked three jobs to keep her family afloat, and the other, the benefits of the weight room, came from Urlacher's assistant coach in high school.

"Brian didn't have much as a kid, and his family lived paycheck to paycheck," says Brandon Ridenour, Urlacher's best friend. "Every role model he has ever had has been a hardworking type who puts

family first, and he knows he's fortunate to have everything he gets."

Urlacher's strong work ethic paid off when an assistant coach of his high school football team suggested he try hitting the weight room around the same time he had a growth spurt. It only took two years for Urlacher to go from a 5-foot-9, 160-pound wide receiver in his sophomore year to a 6-foot-4, 214-pound receiver and free safety in his senior year who led his Lovington, New Mexico, high school football team to a

14–0 record and the state title.

Afterward, only two colleges came calling, and Urlacher accepted a scholarship from the University of New Mexico in 1996, where he was used sparingly in his first two seasons before he was set free in his junior year by his new coach, Rocky Long. With Urlacher's ability to roam the field and attack the ball, he led the country in tackles with 178 in 1998. In his senior year, he added 154 tackles to his career totals, along with 6 touchdown catches and a 15.8-yard punt return average.

IN THE HUDDLE

In 2011, Urlacher's 11th season of 100+ tackles, he broke a tie with Hall of Famer Mike Singletary for the Bears' franchise record. Urlacher also set the single-season team record with 214 tackles in 2002.

The Chicago Bears selected Urlacher with the ninth pick in the 2000 draft, and while they liked what they saw, they had little idea that they'd selected the next Monster of the Midway. Switching permanently to the defensive side of the ball, Urlacher became one in a long line of Bears linebackers who have defined the franchise and stricken fear into opponents.

CAREER HIGHLIGHTS

- Eight-time Pro Bowl selection (2000–2003, 2005, 2006, 2010, 2011)
- Five-time All-Pro (2001, 2002, 2005, 2006, 2010)
- NFL All-Decade Team for the 2000s
- Defensive Player of the Year (2005)
- Defensive Rookie of the Year (2000)
- Consensus All-American (1999)

After a slow start to his rookie year, Urlacher ended up leading the team in tackles while making his first Pro Bowl and being named Defensive Rookie of the Year. Over the next decade, he went on to become the most recognizable, consistent and dominating player on the team, winning the NFL's Defensive Player of the Year award in 2005 and leading the Bears to Super Bowl XLI, a 29–17 loss to the Indianapolis Colts.

Being the leader he is, Urlacher is a player who stands up for his team, but he's also been known to call out his teammates to chide them and spur them on to greater heights. Urlacher's actions have earned him the respect of his team, and they, in turn, have rallied around him during times of trouble, such as when his mother died suddenly in 2011.

"He's been the face of the franchise, sometimes reluctantly," says Bears chairman George McCaskey. "But he's accepted that responsibility. You saw last year how his teammates feel about him when his mom passed away. And you saw how he felt about his teammates when, in the midst of his grief, he came back to his family in the locker room. Just a hell of a guy."

Carrying that grief, Urlacher finished his 11th season with the Bears with over 100 tackles. He also made the Pro Bowl for the eighth time but missed the All-Star scrimmage after spraining his MCL in the fourth quarter of the final game of the season. The game was a meaningless encounter against the Minnesota Vikings, and with both teams out of the playoffs, questions arose as to why Urlacher was played in the first place. As he lay on the field, even Minnesota's fans stood in respectful silence and then gave him a rousing ovation when he walked off. Urlacher, however, likely wouldn't have had it any other way, as missing out on the game would have gone against everything he stands for.

Urlacher is already established in the Monsters of the Midway firmament as the team's all-time leader in total tackles and sacks as a linebacker, and fans are looking forward to 2012, when they are confident Urlacher will be back from his knee injury to pick up where he left off in 2011.

Chicago knows Urlacher's presence is crucial in order for the Bears to have a successful season. "You can't replace a guy like him," says quarterback Jay Cutler. "He's the heart and soul of this team."

DALLAS COWBOYS
LINEBACKER
94

DEMARCUS WARE

While he was a student at Auburn High School in Alabama, DeMarcus Ware hawked soft drinks in the stands at Auburn University football games. A standout on both sides of the ball on his high school team, Ware dreamt of being at the stadium in a Tigers' uniform, not a vendor's.

During his high school years, Ware was a four-sport star, excelling at basketball, baseball, track and football. It was on the gridiron, however, where he really shone, earning nods as most valuable linebacker and wide receiver. He was also recognized as a leader of the team — all while playing with future New York Giants All-Pro and Pro Bowl linebacker Osi Umenyiora.

In the end, Auburn didn't recruit Ware and he ended up at the only college that did — Alabama's Troy University. Success took a few years, but as a senior at Troy, Ware was named a third-team All-American, All-Sun Belt and Sun Belt Defensive Player of the Year. He finished with 53 tackles, 29 pressures, 19 tackles for a loss, a career-high 10.5 sacks and 4 forced fumbles to lead the Trojans to their first bowl appearance, where they lost to Northern Illinois University in the Silicon Valley Classic. Ware was also a finalist for the Ted Hendricks Award, which is given out yearly to the top defensive end in college football.

Even with these accolades, Ware was seen as a "tweener" when he entered the 2005 draft, as he fell somewhere between a defensive end and an outside linebacker. Projected to go in the second round, Cowboys owner Jerry Jones had a little more faith in Ware and insisted Dallas take him in the first round with the 11th overall pick. This proved to be a wise decision by Jones. Ware is one of the league's most explosive and dominant defenders, and since he entered the league, no one has posted more sacks than him. He's had double-digit totals in each of the last six seasons, including an NFL-best 20 in 2008 and 15.5 in 2010, numbers that placed him as just the fifth player to top the league more than once. He also has five of the top-six sack totals in Cowboys history, and has been on the Pro Bowl and All-Pro teams for the past six years.

However, while building his impressive resume and fearsome reputation, Ware was also dealing

CAREER HIGHLIGHTS

• Six-time Pro Bowl selection (2006, 2007, 2008, 2009, 2010, 2011)

• Four-time First Team All-Pro selection (2007, 2008, 2009, 2011)

• Two-time Second Team All-Pro selection (2006, 2010)

• Two-time NFL sack leader (2008, 2010)

• NFC Defensive Player of the Year (2008)

• NFL 2000s All-Decade Team

with emotionally crippling challenges off the field. He and his wife Taniqua suffered three failed pregnancies, including their son Omar, who was stillborn.

IN THE HUDDLE
Since Ware entered the league in 2005, no player has achieved more sacks than his 99.5.

Omar's memory is Ware's inspiration. "I feel Omar out there with me, watching over me and protecting me. Sometimes, when I'm tired on the field, and I feel like I can't go anymore, I just think, what if he had one more breath? What if all three did?"

The Wares have since adopted daughter Marley and in November 2010 welcomed biological son DeMarcus Jr. into the world, and while Taniqua calls DeMarcus Sr. "a big softie" with his kids, he certainly hasn't weakened on the field.

In the 2011 season, Ware was threatening to break Michael Strahan's single-season sack record (22.5), but constant double-teaming wore him down and he fell short with 19.5 — half a sack shy of becoming the first player in NFL history with two 20-sack seasons. The Cowboys also came up short in 2011, losing a must-win game to Umenyiora's Giants on the final day of the season to finish 8–8 and out of the playoffs. Ware was named to the Pro Bowl and First Team All-

Pro at the season's end, however, and at the age of 29 and with four more years on his contract, he is destined to be the anchor of the Cowboys' defense for many seasons to come.

Ware knows nothing in life can be taken for granted, though, and this fact was reinforced in a December 2009 game when Ware was carted off the field on a backboard after his head hit the leg of San Diego Chargers lineman Brandyn Dombrowski. Fortunately, Ware only suffered a sprained neck and was back to work six days later.

"I just didn't think that would be my last play, going out on a stretcher," says Ware. "Usually when guys leave the field like that, it's pretty bad. My destiny, I guess, is to play ball."

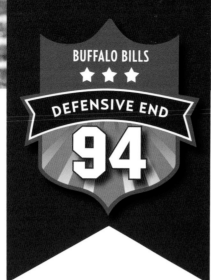

MARIO WILLIAMS

When Mario Williams was growing up, he idolized Barry Sanders and Emmitt Smith and dreamed of being an NFL running back, but now that Williams has fully grown to a chiseled 6-foot-6 and 285 pounds, it's clear that genetics had a different plan for him. As *Muscle & Fitness* magazine once said, "It looks like Mario Williams has baby seals connecting his shoulders to his elbows."

Williams can bench-press 450 pounds, has a 41-inch vertical leap and has enough speed to run the ball if he really wants to. At Richlands High School in North Carolina, he had 590 yards rushing on only 58 carries. However, it was his 87 tackles (including 22 for a loss) and 13 sacks in his senior year that earned him a scholarship to North Carolina State University.

Most of North Carolina's defensive record book was dismantled by Williams in his three years with the Wolfpack, including stops for a loss in a career (55.5) and season (27.5), and sacks in a career (26.5) and season (14.5). He was also named a first-team All-American by the NFL Draft Report and *Sports Illustrated* after his junior year, when he declared for the draft (2006).

Many were shocked when the Texans, only four years into their existence and with a losing record

in each one, didn't pick the biggest name on the board, Heisman winner and college legend Reggie Bush, then a tailback at the University of Southern California. And, if the Texans were going to deviate from expectations, the general assumption was that they would draft local quarterback hero Vince Young from the University of Texas. In the end, they picked Williams first overall.

As Bill Simmons of ESPN.com wrote after the draft, "It's one thing to make a shaky personnel decision, it's another thing to kick your fans in the teeth." Simmons' colleague Len Pasquarelli agreed: "Ladies and gentlemen, your Houston Texans, an outfit that might do better were Mr. Magoo executing its lottery selections."

Six seasons later, it's clear the Texans weren't blind. Both Bush and Young have moved on from the teams that drafted them and are trying to resurrect careers that have been less than spectacular.

Meanwhile, Williams set Houston's single-season team sack record in 2007 with 14.0 and had the franchise career mark after only four seasons. The 2007 campaign was particularly sweet for Williams. His first sack was against the Indianapolis Colts' Peyton Manning, a superstar and division rival the Texans drafted Williams to stop, and he had 2.5 sacks of old nemesis Young in a game against the Tennessee Titans. At one point late in the season, Williams had 55 total

tackles (including sacks, unassisted tackles and assisted tackles) and of those 55 plays, opponents gained a total of 1.5 yards, which is 0.02 yards per play.

IN THE HUDDLE
After just four seasons, Williams held the Texans' franchise record for career sacks; he currently sits at 53.0 for his career.

Williams followed up 2007 with 12.0 more sacks in 2008 and 9.0 in 2009, numbers that led the team and got Williams voted into two of his three Pro Bowls. In 2010, he missed games for the first time in his career because of a sports hernia, but he had surgery on his groin in the off-season and started 2011 strong — in the season opener he had two sacks, two quarterback hurries, a tackle for loss, a forced fumble and a forced intentional-grounding call in the Texans' 34–7 demolition of the

Peyton Manning–less Colts. Unfortunately, Williams later tore his pectoral muscle and was lost for the remainder of the year.

After his shortened season the Texans weren't willing to break the bank to keep him around, and the Buffalo Bills swooped in and signed Williams to a six year deal that could be worth $100 million, the richest contract a defensive player has ever signed. And maybe Buffalo head coach Chan Gailey sweetened the pot by promising him a few chances to run the ball in for a score, the way Chicago Bears coach Mike Ditka did with 380-pound defensive lineman William "The Refrigerator" Perry in Super Bowl XX.

For now, though, Williams is happy to play defense. "Getting a sack is like getting a touchdown," he says. "The crowd goes crazy. It's like you can breathe easy for a minute — it's a breath of fresh air."

PATRICK WILLIS

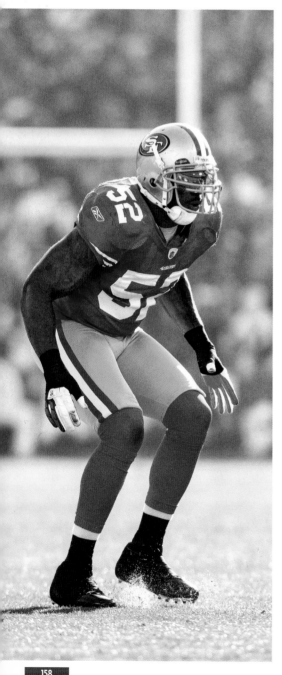

Prior to the 2011 season, the San Francisco 49ers' Patrick Willis was voted the top interior lineman in the NFL by *USA Today.* "He's by far the best linebacker in the game right now," the New York Jets' sixth-ranked David Harris said of Willis. "Look at his numbers, they're ridiculous. Every year, he leads the league in tackles. He's the guy."

Well, not quite every year (Willis has led the league twice), but he does relish his role in the NFL trenches.

"Being a linebacker, it's all about the will not to be denied," Willis says. "You have to be a caveman to do it all — stop the run, stop the pass and be elite. Ain't anything pretty about it. As a middle linebacker, your job is dirty." And Willis knows a thing or two about dirty jobs — growing up in Bruceton, Tennessee, he chopped weeds in cotton fields at age 10 and went on to mix mortar at building sites and wield a chainsaw as a lumberjack.

Willis also waxed the floors of his high school, including the hardcourt where he was a standout basketball player who averaged close to 20 points and 10 rebounds per game. An all-district, all-region and All-West Tennessee selection, he played every position on the court and was named district MVP.

As a child, Patrick, his brother and his dad built a basketball hoop from cedar planks on the dirt in front of their house. "That's what kept me busy. We didn't have sport clubs, malls or movie theaters nearby. All we had was each other," says Willis.

Then, at 16 years old, Willis and his siblings were taken from their father, Ernest, who had been taking drugs and abusing his four children. Willis was adopted by his basketball coach and his wife, Chris and Julie Finley, whom he now refers to as his mother and father.

IN THE HUDDLE

Willis is the first player in 49ers history to be an All-Pro in each of his first five seasons, and he is the first player to win the Butkus Award in both college and in the NFL.

By the time he graduated from high school, Willis had lettered in basketball and baseball, but he chose to focus on football after he dominated both sides of the ball and was nominated as Tennessee's Mr. Football as both a linebacker and tailback.

At the University of Mississippi, Willis narrowed his expertise and stuck with defense. He consequently won the Ole Miss Scholar-Athlete Award as a freshman and was named All-SEC and All-American as a

junior and senior. As a senior, he also won the Butkus Award and the Jack Lambert Award — both of which recognize the top lineman in the nation — and for good measure took home the Conerly Award for being the best college football player in Mississippi.

Willis was the first lineman picked (11th overall, by the 49ers) in the 2007 draft, and by the end of the year he was the NFL leader in tackles (174), which made him the first 49er since Ronnie Lott to be named to the All-Pro and Pro Bowl teams as a rookie.

Four years later and Willis has garnered four more double nominations. "Nobody in the NFL plays their position better than Patrick Willis, and that is saying a lot," says Matt Williamson of Scouts Inc. "He is as good a linebacker as Peyton Manning is a quarterback, as Andre Johnson is a receiver, as

Adrian Peterson is a running back. He has no weaknesses."

Willis, in reality, has at least one small weakness, and it showed in 2011 when he injured his hamstring in a game against the St. Louis Rams, causing him to miss the final three games of the season. Despite the incident, Willis still had the most forced fumbles, fumble recoveries and passes deflected of his career, and while he earned his usual season-ending honors, Willis' greatest achievement in 2011 was helping the 49ers make the playoffs for the first time in his tenure. Case in point: he came back early from injury and fought through the pain to record eight tackles in a win over the New Orleans Saints, and then made eight more — plus a sack and a deflected pass — in an overtime loss to the New York Giants in the NFC Championship.

2011 was also special for Willis

CAREER HIGHLIGHTS

- Five-time Pro Bowl selection (2007–11)
- Five-time All-Pro (2007–11)
- Defensive Rookie of the Year (2007)
- The 49ers' first two-time winner of the Bill Walsh Award (team MVP as voted by San Francisco's coaches)
- Led the NFL in tackles in 2007 and 2009

because it was the first time his biological father Ernest, again a part of his life, saw a live 49ers game, and a week before the NFC final, Willis' two fathers shared a basketball court back in Tennessee. The hope for both men is that after the 2012 season, they will be sitting side-by-side in New Orleans, watching their son dominate the Super Bowl.

DEFENSIVE BACKS

NNAMDI ASOMUGHA — Philadelphia Eagles

CHAMP BAILEY — Denver Broncos

TROY POLAMALU — Pittsburgh Steelers

ED REED— Baltimore Ravens

DARRELLE REVIS — New York Jets

GEORGE WILSON — Buffalo Bills

CHARLES WOODSON — Green Bay Packers

NNAMDI ASOMUGHA

One of the main reasons why football is America's most popular sport is because of the nation's propensity for betting on games and organizing fantasy football leagues — according to *Adweek* magazine, some 27 million Americans are in a fantasy football league, and 5.4 million of them are women. The appetite for football statistics appears insatiable, which makes Philadelphia Eagles cornerback Nnamdi Asomugha a bit of an enigma.

IN THE HUDDLE

One of the most philanthropic players in the NFL, Asomugha discussed community service as part of Bill Clinton's Global Initiative, provides aid to widows and orphans in Nigeria and helps them become independent through education and vocational training, and he takes inner-city high school students to universities and colleges to encourage the pursuit of higher education.

Despite being recognized as one of the best in the game, Asomugha doesn't really have the stats to back up his reputation. However, there's a simple explanation: opposing quarterbacks don't throw the ball in Asomugha's direction because it will probably end up as an incompletion or interception. Asomugha doesn't put up gaudy numbers, but neither do the star receivers he covers.

Asomugha is also unique among NFL players because of his upbringing. Asomugha grew up in the Los Angeles area after his parents emigrated from Nigeria to earn doctorates, but he always felt like the underachiever in an accomplished family.

"It was a subtle pressure I put on myself. It can be a bit sententious in the Nigerian household, to the point where you feel like with any wrong step you've set yourself back so far. It's like everything has to be done right. I was always the person who would make the mistake. I was the one who would get suspended from school. No one else was getting those things, so I felt like there was a problem with me. 'What's wrong with me?'"

Being taken out of sports by his parents until he buckled down academically helped motivate Asomugha, and he finished high school with an excellent grade point average and a football scholarship to the University of California, Berkeley, where

he earned his B.A. in Finance — a useful degree to have after becoming the NFL's highest paid player in 2008.

A payday of that caliber seemed unlikely after Asomugha was drafted 31st overall by the Oakland Raiders in 2003. Playing behind stars Charles Woodson and Phillip Buchanon, Asomugha didn't see much of the field in his first two seasons, and critics were calling him a first-round bust. However, once he got his chance to shine, everyone changed their tune.

Asomugha earned a starting position in the 2005 season, and his first game was against the defending Super Bowl champions, the New England Patriots. Tom Brady picked on the young cornerback all day, and afterward, Asomugha questioned his ability and his future. Older brother Chijioke, a former corner at Stanford, reminded him after the game that he was thrust into the spotlight by Brady, for better or worse, and given a platform by the NFL so he could do something special.

"When you realize that, your whole mind-set changes," Asomugha says. "Your determination changes, your goals, the zest that you put into each day changes, because now you're realizing that you're not just here for no reason. You're here to make a mark. I kid you not — from that game forward I feel like I've gotten better every game I've played."

By the 2007 season, Asomugha was a team captain and opposing quarterbacks tested him just 31 times for 10 completions the entire season. An NFL scout said he was thrown at "less than any defender in the last 10 years."

Asomugha's 2008 season was even quieter, with 27 passes sent his way and just eight completed. Only All-Pros Randy Moss (3 receptions, 40 yards) and Tony Gonzalez (2 receptions, 34 yards) had more than one catch against Asomugha, and he didn't allow a touchdown the entire season.

Probably the most coveted free agent entering the 2011 season and one of several marquee names the Eagles signed when the lockout ended, Asomugha agreed to a five-year, $60 million contract with Philadelphia. The "Dream Team," as they were dubbed, ended up having a nightmare season, with a record of 8–8 and an early vacation instead of a trip to the Super Bowl.

After being asked to play new positions in the backfield and learning a new system without the benefit of a full training camp, Asomugha had an off year by his own lofty standards, but a player with his athletic gifts and intelligence will master them and continue to have quiet games on the stat sheet — and so will the opposing receivers. Fantasy football players who underestimate him in 2012 and offensive coordinators who choose to throw in Asomugha's general direction will do so at their own peril.

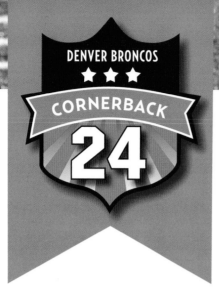

CHAMP BAILEY

Roland Bailey has been known as "Champ" since his mother gave him the nickname as a child, and even though it's been a grand name to live up to, Bailey has taken it all in stride.

At Charlton County High, in Folkston, Georgia, Bailey racked up a whopping 5,855 total yards and 394 points as a running back and quarterback. He also had 80 tackles, 8 interceptions and 4 fumble recoveries on defense, and was named an All-State player.

IN THE HUDDLE

Bailey's 11 Pro Bowl selections are the most by any cornerback in NFL history, and he's one shy of tying the all-time record held by Randall McDaniel and Will Shields.

Bailey took his multitasking skills to the University of Georgia, where he averaged 103.5 all-purpose yards a game and was in on 957 total plays (547 defense, 301 offense and 109 special teams) during his collegiate career. He was a consensus All-American and won the Bronko Nagurski Award as the top defensive player in the country in his junior season before declaring for the draft a year early.

Chosen seventh overall in the 1999 draft by the Washington Redskins, Bailey started all 16 games of his rookie year and had 5 interceptions and 83 tackles. Over the next four seasons in Washington he had 13 total interceptions as a cornerback, while also playing on special teams and as a wide receiver, and was named to the Pro Bowl each year.

Heading into the 2004 season, Bailey was due for a raise and was not thrilled with an impending franchise tag. He threatened to hold out, and in a surprising move, the Redskins gave him permission to seek a trade. The Denver Broncos indulged Washington, and in gaining Bailey, swapped running back Clinton Portis and a second-round pick.

This was the same year the NFL started enforcing illegal-contact rules, which, by banning contact five yards beyond the line of scrimmage, severely limited the physical obstruction defenders could have with receivers. Cornerbacks were vulnerable to being burned for big plays, but Bailey was not one of them.

In his three previous seasons, Bailey had only eight interceptions because teams simply didn't throw in his direction, but, emboldened by the new rules, opponents attacked him again. He had three interceptions in 2004 and once he got more comfortable with the new reality in 2005 he made them pay with a team-record five-game interception streak and eight on the season.

Bailey followed that up with a career-high 98 tackles and 10

interceptions in 2006, which tied him for the league lead. He also placed second in Defensive Player of the Year voting.

By 2010, Bailey was a member of the NFL's All-Decade team, but, creeping into his 30s, Bailey wondered if his days were numbered. Executive vice president and former quarterback John Elway, however, made sure Bailey stayed in the Mile High City, signing him to a contract worth more than $40 million that will keep him in Denver through the 2014 season.

"Champ is truly one of the NFL's elite players, a 10-time Pro Bowler who is playing at the absolute highest level," said Elway. "He demands greatness from himself at all times and is going to play a big part in returning the Broncos to championship contention."

In 2011, Bailey went over 700 career tackles, caught his 50th career interception and was named to his 11th Pro Bowl team. Additionally, the Broncos, picked by experts to

finish out of the playoff picture that year, upset the Pittsburgh Steelers in the first round but ran out of steam against the New England Patriots in the second round.

This was the Broncos' first trip to the postseason since 2006, when, against the defending champion Patriots, Bailey executed one of the signature plays of his career. He intercepted a Tom Brady pass and returned it 100 yards, which is the longest non-scoring play in NFL postseason history. Bailey's dash set up the game-sealing touchdown, which handed Brady his first career postseason loss and sent the Broncos to the AFC Championship game.

Bailey's play certainly earned Brady's respect: "He's one of the very best in the history of the league at playing cornerback. He plays well against all styles of receivers, too. It's not like you go in there saying, 'Let's figure out if Champ can beat us,' because he usually can."

"As a pro athlete, you live for these moments," said Bailey

CAREER HIGHLIGHTS

- Eleven-time Pro Bowl selection (2000–2007, 2009–2011)
- Six-time All-Pro (2000, 2003–2007)
- NFL All-Decade Team for the 2000s
- Denver Broncos 50th Anniversary Team
- Bronko Nagurski Award (1998)
- Consensus All-American (1998)

afterward. "This is why you play, to be on the big stage and get out there and show what we can do as a team. That's what motivates me to keep playing this game."

With the addition of Peyton Manning at quarterback for the 2012 season, Denver could finally have the horses to win the Super Bowl for the first time since before Bailey began his Hall of Fame career. Enshrinement is ensured, living up to his moniker remains the elusive goal that spurs him on.

PITTSBURGH STEELERS
★ ★ ★
SAFETY
43

TROY
POLAMALU

All professional athletes have insurance, and some even have specific body parts insured, but the Pittsburgh Steelers' Troy Polamalu takes it to another level — he has his hair insured.

In fairness to Polamalu, he wasn't the one who insured his flowing black mane; the shampoo company he endorses took out the $1 million Lloyd's of London policy on his locks, and because of the combination of an abundance of hair and memorable TV commercials, Polamalu is one of the most recognizable athletes in America today.

Born in California and raised in Oregon by his mother's Samoan family, Troy Aumua Polamalu is more than just a hairdo. He has been a whirlwind on the football field ever since he started throwing his 5-foot-8, 135-pound body around as a high school freshman.

Polamalu followed up his high school days at the University of Southern California (USC), where he was a hybrid player, covering both safety positions and foreshadowing his professional future. As a Trojan, he had 278 total tackles — including 29 behind the line of scrimmage — 6 interceptions, 13 pass deflections and 4 blocked punts. He was also first-team All Pac-10 twice and named Most Inspirational Player by his teammates.

"I've never coached a player with his passion," said Greg Burns, Polamalu's position coach during his senior year at USC. "He wasn't vocal, but he was relentless."

Therein lays the Polamalu dichotomy. He's a ball of fury on the field but self-effacing and cerebral off it. His hobbies are surfing, playing piano, gardening and making furniture. He's also a devout Greek Orthodox Christian and religious scholar who doesn't watch football at home.

"You watch him play, and he's this true warrior," says Buffalo Bills quarterback Ryan Fitzpatrick. "And then you shake hands with him on the field afterward, and he talks so softly that you can hardly hear him."

IN THE HUDDLE
Polamalu is immortalized as a wax figure at Madame Tussauds in New York, where his likeness was created using extra-long human hair that was specially ordered and permed.

Polamalu is known for blitzing from the line of scrimmage, defending passes 50 yards into the secondary and roaming sideline to sideline in a freelancing role that's borne as much of film study as it is from instinct and speed.

"There's no defensive player in the history of the NFL who has had the freedom Troy Polamalu has right now," says Rodney Harrison, former All-Pro safety and current NBC analyst.

"What that really means is that I have more freedom than anybody else to make mistakes," explains Polamalu. "And then my teammates cover them up. You wouldn't believe how many mistakes I make."

CAREER HIGHLIGHTS
- Seven-time Pro Bowl selection (2004–2008, 2010, 2011)
- Five-time All Pro (2004, 2005, 2008, 2010, 2011)
- Defensive Player of the Year (2010)
- Steelers MVP and Man of the Year (2010)
- Two-time Super Bowl champion (XL, XLIII)
- Named to the NFL All-Decade Team for the 2000s and the Steelers' 75th Season All-Time Team

The mistakes, though, appear to be few and far between, and the results speak for themselves. Polamalu was instrumental in the Steelers winning Super Bowls XL and XLIII, he has made seven Pro Bowl and five All-Pro teams and he was the Defensive Player of the Year in 2010. He also does things on the field that no one sees coming.

Tennessee Titans quarterback Kerry Collins can attest to that. In 2010, Polamalu made possibly the most memorable play of his career when, with the Titans lined up on the Steelers' one-yard line, he timed the snap perfectly and just as the ball made it to Collins' hands, he leapt over guard Leroy Harris before anyone else had moved to sack Collins. The play made every highlight reel as much for its innovation as for its athleticism.

Approaching the game with such abandon exacts a toll, and the 5-foot-10, 207-pound Polamalu is no stranger to the trainer's room; he missed 21

games between 2006 and 2010 and has a history of concussions.

"He gets hurt all the time, he gets concussions, his shoulder gets bent out of shape, but you can't keep him off the field. He's not that big, not that fast, but he's everywhere and everyone needs to know where he is when they line up," says Hall of Fame running back Floyd Little.

Before the 2011 season, Polamalu was due to enter the final year of the contract he signed in 2007, and the Steelers were confident enough in Polamalu's abilities, health and future to offer him an extension. But, in keeping with the team's policy of not negotiating during the season, they signed him (through 2014) at the airport on the eve of the opener.

It was money well spent — Polamalu played every game in 2011 and was again named to the Pro Bowl and All-Pro teams. And, while it's true that Polamalu's signature locks now have a touch of gray, he's still head and shoulders above the rest.

BALTIMORE RAVENS
★ ★ ★
SAFETY
20

ED REED

Ed Reed is already a member of the Hall of Fame … the one at Destrehan High School that sits on the banks of the Mississippi in Louisiana. This path to sports glory was set in motion during Reed's junior year when he asked his school's secretary, Jeanne Hall, if he could move in with her. Hall was a guardian to many of the school's troubled kids, and while Reed had supportive parents, each of them worked long hours to take care of their five boys. Reed's parents consented to his altered living arrangements in order to provide a better place for him to do his homework and to avoid trouble.

"There was something inside of me that [the Halls] brought out," Reed says. "And once I realized what I could do, I wanted to take it to another level. I saw if I did things right, people would follow me."

Reed worked hard both during and after school; he played on the basketball team and track team (for which he threw the javelin and ran the 4x100 relay), as well as played on the football team. He was a defensive back and quarterback and returned kicks for the team, and was named All-State his senior year.

Heavily recruited, Reed chose the University of Miami, where he was a consensus All-American in his junior and senior years. He was also co-captain when the Hurricanes won the national championship in 2001.

IN THE HUDDLE
Reed has scored 13 touchdowns in his career (including playoffs) and is the only player in NFL history to score return touchdowns from a punt return, blocked punt, interception and fumble recovery.

The following year, Reed was drafted 24th overall by the Baltimore Ravens. As a rookie, he led the team with five interceptions, and he also had the franchise's first two blocked punts, one of which he ran back for a touchdown. Reed kept up the pace the following season — avoiding the sophomore slump, he set the Ravens' franchise record with seven interceptions. He also made his first Pro Bowl.

In 2004, however, Reed truly brake out as a football star. He led the league with 9 interceptions and returned them for an NFL-record 358 yards. He also made 89

CAREER HIGHLIGHTS

- Eight-time Pro Bowl selection (2003, 2004, 2006–2011)

- Eight-time All-Pro (2003, 2004, 2006–2011)

- Three-time NFL interception leader (2004, 2008, 2010)

- Defensive Player of the Year (2004)

- NFL All-Decade Team for the 2000s

- Has the two longest interception returns in NFL history (106 yards versus Cleveland in 2004 and 107 yards versus Philadelphia in 2008)

tackles and was named Defensive Player of the Year, which was only the third time a safety had won the honor in the 34-year history of the award.

With 57 career interceptions under his belt, Reed is now the franchise and active NFL leader; he is also the active NFL leader in postseason interceptions (8) and has the highest interception return average in NFL history (25.7 yards).

"He's the best safety in the league," says a rival personnel director. "His instincts, the way he positions himself, his ability to close on the ball — all those qualities are unusual for a safety. And he's a terrific runner after an interception."

In the first game of the 2011 season, Reed broke Ronnie Lott's

NFL record with 12 career games with multiple interceptions, and at the end of the year Reed was only 21 yards short of Rod Woodson's all-time interception return yards record — even though, at that point, Reed had played 94 fewer games than Woodson.

Reed will likely beat Woodson's record while in a Ravens uniform, so the question becomes not how he will break it, but how far he will take the record and for whom. Reed is 34 years old and heading into the final year of his contract. Yes, he played 16 games in 2011, but his effectiveness was limited by a shoulder injury. Reed has pondered retirement in the past, specifically in 2008 when nerve problems in his neck and shoulder started to bother him and in 2010

when he suffered a torn labrum in his hip. These maladies, however, only served to illuminate Reed's importance to the Ravens — in 6 games without him, the team had 3 interceptions, and in the 10 games with him, they had 16.

In light of his continued success, Reed believes there's a divine plan in place for his football future, and as recently as 2012, he told the appreciative crowd at his University of Miami Hall of Fame induction that he intends to play NFL football for another four or five years.

But, when Reed finally does call it quits, the "unique, once-in-a-lifetime football player" (according to former Ravens defensive coordinator Greg Mattison) can almost certainly book his ticket to Canton for a Hall of Fame hat trick.

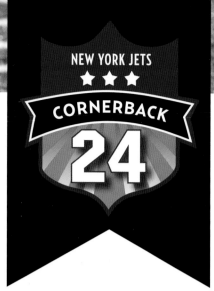

NEW YORK JETS
★ ★ ★
CORNERBACK
24

DARRELLE REVIS

Rikers Island is a notorious prison where New York City's hardened criminals go for a time out and to think about what they have done; "Revis Island" is a mythical purgatory where the New York Jets' opponents go to be alone and accomplish little. The "residents" of the island are the NFL's best receivers, and they are stranded by the 5-foot-11, 198-pound warden known as the shutdown cornerback with the impressive agility, speed, vision and instincts.

Growing up in Aliquippa, Pennsylvania, inside a 13-room home where four generations of his family lived, Darrelle Revis could see past the rundown rows of houses to the bleachers of Aliquippa High School, where the whole town gathered on Friday nights to watch the football team. This is where he ended up owning the field as a quarterback, wide receiver, defensive back and kick returner. In his senior year in 2003, Revis averaged 15.4 yards per touch and scored 14

touchdowns in 5 playoff games, including 5 in the state final, and was named Pennsylvania Player of the Year.

After high school, Revis chose to further his education and take his chance at football stardom. He attended the University of Pittsburgh, where he focused on defense and completed a three-year career with 129 tackles, 8 interceptions and 4 touchdowns (2 from interceptions and 2 on punt returns) before skipping his senior

CAREER HIGHLIGHTS

- Four-time Pro Bowl selection (2008–2011)
- Three-time All-Pro (2009–2011)
- AFC Defensive Player of the Year (2009)
- All-Rookie Team (2007)

season to enter the NFL draft.

The Jets chose Revis 14th overall in 2007 after trading first-, second- and fifth–round draft picks to the Carolina Panthers in order to move up and get their star one spot ahead of his hometown Pittsburgh Steelers.

The Jets knew they were getting an elite cornerback, but they didn't realize they were also getting a workaholic. Revis obsessively studies film, learning the tendencies and tells of the receivers he will face. He takes this a step further by tailoring specific workouts to combat his opponents, and in the off-season he hauls truck tires, pulls sleds and runs up mountains in the Arizona heat.

"He just attacks his job," says Jets coach Rex Ryan. "If there is one guy I want to cover somebody, with my paycheck on it, I want it to be Darrelle Revis."

Ryan almost had to put his own money down — after Revis' first All-Pro and second Pro Bowl selection in 2009, he held out to have his contract restructured.

Jets receiver and practice nemesis Braylon Edwards was thrilled when Revis re-signed just before the 2010 season began. "You can tell that the energy is definitely different around with Darrelle back. And why wouldn't it be? Getting a great player back — the best defensive back, and maybe the best defensive player, in the NFL — it's just huge for us."

Revis had another Pro Bowl and All-Pro season in 2010, and he led

the Jets to their second consecutive AFC Championship appearance, a 24–19 loss to the Steelers in which Revis had eight tackles and a pass deflection.

IN THE HUDDLE

In 2006, Revis was a finalist for the Jim Thorpe Award and won ESPN's College Football Play of the Year accolades for a thrilling 73-yard punt-return touchdown.

Prior to the 2011 season, ESPN graded and ranked every player in the NFL. Revis was tied at the top with quarterbacks Tom Brady and Peyton Manning and running back Adrian Peterson. Ryan agreed with ESPN's assessment: "Revis is the best player in football. It doesn't matter — mid-season, postseason, whatever. There's only one Darrelle Revis in this league, and we're fortunate to

have him. If we choose to lock him down on somebody, it's probably going to be a long afternoon for that player."

Revis lived up to expectations in 2011 with 52 tackles, 21 passes defended and 4 interceptions, including one he returned 100 yards for a touchdown against the Miami Dolphins. The Jets stumbled, though, and missed the playoffs with an 8–8 record.

No man, however, is an island, and as the Jets' best player, the soft-spoken Revis will have to step up and take more of a leadership role in 2012 in order to bring discipline to a locker room that even he admits was in "disarray" in 2011.

"When I was growing up, I looked at the people who made it to the NFL," Revis says. "But I wanted to be better than them. I wanted to surpass them. Now, it's my time."

GEORGE WILSON

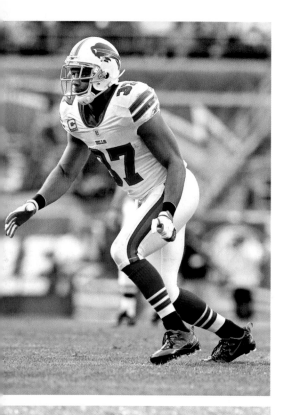

CAREER HIGHLIGHTS

- Buffalo Bills Walter Payton Man of the Year Award (2009)

- Voted team captain for four consecutive seasons

- Had career highs in tackles (91), sacks (2) and interceptions (4) in 2009

- The second Bills defensive back to record consecutive multi-sack seasons (after Lawyer Milloy)

In the one-on-one battles that decide NFL games, Buffalo Bills strong safety George Wilson has a unique advantage in knowing his enemies. A star wideout in high school and college, he made the rare transition to defense after cracking the Bills roster as a receiver. It might explain why, after never playing a down as a safety before he reached the NFL, he's now one of the best in the league.

A two-time All-State wide receiver at Tilghman High School in Paducah, Kentucky, and a finalist for Kentucky Male Athlete of the Year, Wilson was a heavily recruited prospect. He chose to attend the University of Arkansas in 2000, where he went into the Razorbacks' record books for being second in career receptions and third in receiving yards. His best collegiate game was against Kentucky State University, with 172 yards and a touchdown on nine receptions in a 71–63 overtime win.

Wilson also learned a valuable lesson from his Arkansas position coach James Shibest, who told him he had to focus on becoming a great football player, not just a great receiver. It was a lesson Wilson took to heart when then Bills head coach Dick Jauron approached Wilson about becoming a safety after the 2006 season.

"To be a part of a team you have to truly put the team first and make sacrifices," says Wilson. "If this meant that I needed to learn an entirely new position and say goodbye to the one that I had worked on for so many years, then that is what the team needed."

It's not like Wilson had been setting the league on fire on the offensive side of the ball. After going undrafted he signed with the Detroit Lions as a free agent in 2004, and then was signed to the Bills' practice squad later that year. His first NFL game was in September 2005 against the Houston Texans, and it was one of three games in three years he played without a reception.

IN THE HUDDLE
Wilson was in the videos for Mary J. Blige's "We Got Hood Love" and Marsha Ambrosius' "Late Nights & Early Mornings."

Wilson spent the summer before the 2007 season learning how to play safety, and he didn't waste any time in showing off his new tricks on the big stage. "My first NFL start was on

Monday Night Football against the Cowboys, the team I grew up watching in my living room, and I hadn't made a catch or clearly ever scored a touchdown in the NFL after years as a wide receiver. On the third play of the game Tony Romo overthrew Jason Witten and I intercepted it and took it in for a touchdown. It was a little piece of heaven; 8 to 10 seconds of joy after 16 years of hard work. It was all worth it."

Wilson played in 12 games as a safety that year and, going forward, became a fixture in the Bills' defensive backfield, recording career highs in tackles (91), sacks (2) and interceptions (4) in 2009.

Early in the 2011 season, it looked like the Bills were on their way to the playoffs, with Wilson an integral cog. In an October game against the heavily favored Philadelphia Eagles, Wilson had 11 solo tackles, an interception and three pass deflections in a 31–24 Buffalo victory. He also won the AFC Defensive Player of the Week award and helped the Bills to a 4–1 record. The next month, he had already surpassed his career high in tackles when he suffered a neck injury against the Dallas Cowboys on November 13 and ended up missing three games. Star running back Fred Jackson was also lost to a broken leg, and the Bills' season hit the skids.

Wilson, however, knows the team has the potential to be among the NFL elite again, and he believes the faith of Buffalo fans will be rewarded. "This city deserves a winner. I truly believe that Coach [Chan] Gailey and [general manager] Buddy Nix are building this organization the right way and we're moving in that direction. It's going to come. That day is going to be full of joy. I dream about it all the time. I know a lot of them [fans] dream about it. We're just so appreciative of their love and their commitment to our team and their sacrifices."

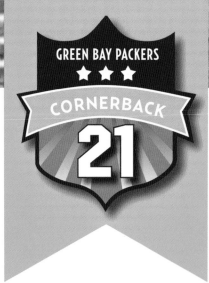

GREEN BAY PACKERS

★ ★ ★

CORNERBACK

21

CHARLES WOODSON

Prior to the 2011 season, the majority of preseason pundits ranked Green Bay Packers cornerback Charles Woodson highly in comparison to his counterparts around the league. The praise, however, was generally qualified with the mention of a lost step or the fact that Woodson is in his mid-30s.

Woodson, however, has made a habit out of defying logic and expectations. For instance, at Ross High School in Fremont, Ohio, he was named the state's "Mr. Football" after setting school records for rushing yards (3,861) and points (466), but after graduation the All-American selection decided to flip to the other side of the ball and become a cornerback with the University of Michigan.

It proved to be a wise decision. Woodson beat out favorite Peyton Manning for the Heisman Trophy in 1997, becoming the first and (still) the only primarily defensive player to win the award. As a Wolverine, he also staked his claim against archrival Ohio State with commanding performance: a 78-yard punt return for a touchdown, a 37-yard pass reception and a drive-killing interception, all in what was Michigan's 11th straight victory on the way to an undefeated season.

In 1998, after winning the Heisman and the national championship with the Wolverines in his junior year, he declared himself eligible for the draft and was picked fourth overall by the Oakland Raiders. He went on to make the Pro Bowl four times with the Raiders and was instrumental in getting the team to Super Bowl XXXVII, which the team lost to the Tampa Bay Buccaneers. Woodson played this game with a fracture in his leg. After playing only six games for the Raiders in 2005, Woodson began hearing whispers that he was over the hill and that he would never fully recover from his broken leg.

In the end, Green Bay was the only team that pursued Woodson when he became a free agent after the 2005 season. He was originally hesitant about the city and its team, but beggars can't be choosers, and he soon put down roots, growing to love the smallest town in professional sports and its obsession with all things green and yellow.

In Woodson's first season with Green Bay, he achieved a career high with eight interceptions, tops

in the NFC, and in the following years has been both remarkable and dependable.

In 2009, Woodson became the first defender to win the Player of the Month award three times and was the oldest defensive back to win Defensive Player of the Year. In 2010, he established new career highs in tackles (115) and forced fumbles (5), and became the first player in league history to return an interception for a touchdown in five straight seasons.

IN THE HUDDLE

A mobile app lets visitors to the C.S. Mott Children's Hospital at the University of Michigan see a 3-D Woodson; the lobby was named after him in honor of his $2 million donation.

That season, Woodson also added the one piece of hardware that had eluded him — the Super Bowl champion's Vince Lombardi Trophy. Yes, he had to watch the second half from the sideline after breaking his collarbone while successfully defending a pass late in the second quarter, but his three tackles in the first half and impassioned speech at halftime spurred the Packers to the title.

Even with the step that critics claim had abandoned Woodson, he still tied for the league lead in interceptions and made both the All-Pro and Pro Bowl teams in 2011 for the seventh and eighth time, respectively. He has also intercepted more than twice as many passes with the Packers (37) than he did in his celebrated time with the Raiders (17).

"In this league they bring in younger guys all the time to either replace you or beat you," Woodson says. "For me just to stick around, I have to get better every year."

And he has, setting an example for the team's younger defenders. "He's the wise one, and the young, hungry guys are falling in line behind the leader," says Green Bay safety Nick Collins.

In 2010, the Packers had enough faith in Woodson's ability to extend his contract for two years on top of the three he had remaining at the time, and when the 35-year-old does eventually retire, he can settle down in Napa Valley and focus on the TwentyFour by Charles Woodson wine he introduced in 2008 but is forbidden from endorsing by the NFL's alcohol policy. After all, Woodson does know a thing or two about getting better with age.

CAREER HIGHLIGHTS

• Eight-time Pro Bowl selection (1998–2001, 2008–11)

• Seven-time All-Pro (1999–2001, 2008–11)

• Super Bowl XLV champion

• Defensive Player of the Year (2009)

• NFL All-Decade Team for the 2000s

• Heisman Trophy winner and national champion (1997)

Acknowledgments

Firefly Books and Steve Cameron, for his gentle but firm guidance.

Stephanie King, Scott Berchtold and the Buffalo Bills, for letting me get up close and personal with the NFL.

My family, for the love and belief.

Friends — Jay, Vik, Brent, Craig, Geoff, Laura, Christine, Claudine, Leslie, Miguel, Debra, Melissa, John, Jen, Nick, Stu, Amelie, Fabian, Paul — for their support, understanding and ribbing.

Donal, for briefly acting as my agent/manager/lawyer.

The Imperials, for being the best team in all of sports.

The players — especially the ones who recognize their position comes with responsibility — for the inspiration, the sacrifices they make and the escape they provide.

Walter Payton, for being larger than life and making a young boy love the game of football.

PROFILE INDEX